General Editors' Preface

The books in this series provide information and advice on a wide range of educational issues for teachers who are busy, yet who are concerned to keep abreast of new developments.

The aim is practicality: slim volumes that are sources of authoritative help and swift reference, written and edited by people whose expertise in their field is backed up by experience of the everyday realities of school and classroom. The books are planned to cover well-defined topics relevant to schools in widely differing situations: subject teaching, curriculum development, areas of responsibility within schools, and the relationship of the school to the community. They are published at a time when there is a growing call for increased professional accountability in our primary and secondary schools. The 'in-service between covers' that characterizes these handbooks is designed to contribute to the vitality and development of schools and of the individuals within them.

This volume comes at a time when there is an increasing realization on the part of practising teachers, the Inspectorate, enlightened employers and others that among the most useful functions of the teacher is to develop the ability of young people to deal with and organize information. The skills covered in *Teaching Information Skills in the Primary School* should be seen as vital for pupils to be able to make the most of educational opportunities at all levels and become independent learners in preparation for life after school. Pat Avann and her contributors describe their experiences, achievements and disappointments, and leave us in no doubt that even the youngest pupil in our primary schools can master tasks that are fundamental to 'learning how to learn'.

Teachers of all years and all subjects in primary schools will find here a wealth of practical guidance and detailed case studies in the acquisition and use of information skills. Head teachers and others responsible for curricular policy will find convincing evidence of the potential of school-wide initiatives, and useful advice on their innovation.

Contributors

Wendy Bloom   Lecturer,
St. Mary's College,
Strawberry Hill,
Twickenham, *formerly*
Teacher,
Cashmore Middle School,
Leamington Spa.

Diana Davies   Deputy Head,
Stoke Infants School,
Coventry.

Marion Griffin   Freelance researcher for the
National Foundation for Educational Research.

Martin Jackson   Head,
St. Nicholas Combined School,
Kenilworth.
Consultant editor *Primary Teaching and Micros*,
Scholastic publications (Magazines) Ltd.

Ann Lewis   Lecturer,
University of Warwick, *formerly*
Deputy Head,
Castle ESN(M) School,
Walsall.

Pauline Millward   Deputy Head,
Delves Junior School,
Walsall.

Contents

1 Introduction: the concern with information skills   1
  Pat Avann

2 Introducing information skills in the infant school   7
  Diana Davies

3 Information skills for children with learning difficulties   27
  Ann Lewis

4 Information skills through project work   43
  Wendy Bloom

5 Problem solving   61
  Pauline Millward

6 Integrating the microcomputer into information skills teaching   77
  Martin Jackson

7 Managing innovation: results of an investigation   91
  Marion Griffin

8 Summing up   108
  Pat Avann

References   110

Bibliography   113

1

Introduction: the concern with information skills

Pat Avann

'How do I teach information skills?' This is a question which primary teachers ask with increasing frequency. It reflects the current concern that learning to learn is not something that develops automatically as children progress through school. Like most questions concerned with education, it does not have one simple answer, but raises other questions in its turn. What are information skills? Can they be taught as a 'subject' or through a series of exercises? How can they become part of the primary curriculum? How do they relate to topic work? At what stage should we begin to teach them? What about the children who experience learning difficulties?

This book sets out to provide some possible answers to these questions, by relating what some teachers have tried in their own classrooms, why they considered action was necessary, their thoughts when looking back on their work, and their ideas for future developments.

In recent years, the idea that children should become independent, flexible learners has found expression in a movement towards resource based learning. Teachers have been encouraged to move away from a rigid, subject-based curriculum and rote learning. They have been seen as the creators of opportunities for children to discover ideas and facts for themselves from a variety of sources such as books, audiovisual aids and outside visits. However, both teachers' own perceptions and some research studies (e.g. 1, 2) suggest that children often leave our schools without the ability to find and evaluate information. Perhaps this is because the attempt to develop autonomy in learning emphasized new teaching methods and the creation of teaching materials as a means of achieving its aims. There was less attention paid to the skills which children need to become successful gatherers, evaluators and users of information. Now it seems there is recognition that a body of 'information skills' does exist which underpins independence in learning, and that such skills need to be identified and developed by teachers.

Defining information skills

The term 'information skills' is not yet widely used. In primary schools 'reference skills' or 'higher order skills' are often used, although 'study skills' seems to be gaining in popularity. To my mind 'study skills' could be identified too closely with the idea of preparation solely for academic work. 'Information skills', in which I would include computer skills, suggests a continuing usefulness after schooling ends.

I would define information skills as those skills concerned with the acquiring of knowledge from a variety of sources, and the ability to assess and apply the information gained. Therefore they certainly include:

1) identifying a need for information and being able to articulate that need (what do I want to know?)
2) framing appropriate questions (how can I find out?)
3) finding information sources (where do I find out?)
4) evaluating information sources (will they answer my questions? How reliable are they?)
5) extracting relevant information (this is what I need to know)
6) processing and, if necessary, presenting the information found to satisfy the original need or to convince others (this is what I've found out).

Such skills will include library skills; comprehension; reading strategies, such as skimming and scanning; identifying main ideas; notetaking; report or essay writing; and, when appropriate to the presentation or understanding of information, mapping and number skills.

Links with language development

Many information skills are linked with reading and language development. The Bullock report and Vera Southgate's study *Extending Beginning Reading* (3) expressed the view that the notable successes achieved in teaching reading should be developed to ensure inferential as well as literal comprehension. Some teachers feel unsure about how to accomplish this and have turned to commercially prepared workcards for assistance. Examples like the *Directions* series (4) and SRA Research Laboratory (5) concentrate on skimming and scanning, finding main ideas, developing library skills and improving comprehension. However, they are often used as exercises, isolated from other classroom activities and their purpose or application to other areas of work is not made clear either to the children or the teacher. Consequently, any skills learned are not transferred, for example, to topic work, which should present an opportunity to develop and practise information skills.

Topic work

My observations of topic work, and discussions with teachers reveal that we share a feeling of disappointment that much work done by children is little more than copying from books. Perhaps the trouble is that the *product* of topic work — the written and illustrated account — has been seen as more important than the *process* by which the information presented is obtained. As soon as attention is directed to *how* children attempt to find information and reprocess it in their own words, the need for the teaching of information skills becomes apparent. I would suggest that the planning of topic work should be started from the idea that the skills which it will develop are at least as important as the subject chosen for study. The steps necessary for progressing through the assignment are:

> what do I want to know?
> what do I already know?
> how can I find out?

These help to define which skills will be necessary at each stage and the adequacy or otherwise of the sources to be consulted (6).

Developing information skills

The ability to learn has been demonstrated and put into practice before children even arrive at school (7). Our task is to channel this ability into school work. Before schooling begins, children learn from what they see and what they are told. As their literacy and knowledge of language widens, we can encourage them, at home and at school, to include books, audiovisual aids and computer databases to expand their ways of learning. This expansion should include the recognition that different information sources are appropriate at different times − a picture is often 'worth a thousand words', and that books or other sources are not infallible, and more than one should be consulted where possible. Children may often be developing such realizations for themselves as they become aware of the conflicting opinions of teachers, parents and classmates! We need to develop flexible learners who will recognize that no one source or method of study is 'best' for everyone, but that any one may be 'best' for an individual pupil or task.

There are, of course, levels of difficulty within the skills and some (such as notetaking) may be better developed later in the junior rather than in the infant classroom.

However, the experiences of infant teachers show that the teaching of information skills can and should *begin* with infants, and Chapters 2 and 3 in this book illustrate what can be achieved. Ways in which the skills can be taught include reinforcement of the alphabet; using dictionaries; developing confidence in identifying books which are relevant to a particular question, and laying the foundations for computer skills.

The successful acquisition of information skills makes demands on teachers as well as children. We need to define and practise them in order to share them. Therefore, there is a need for help in teaching about them in initial and in-service education. The role of the LEA adviser can be an important one in recognizing this need and organizing courses at a local level. This has certainly been the experience of at least two of the writers. The role of the head is also extremely important, as Marion Griffin points out in her chapter. If 'whole school policies', which I believe to be crucial in teaching information skills, are to be adopted, then the head must play a key role in persuading all the teachers in a school to participate. Conversely, lack of support from a head can cause individual teachers' initiatives to fail, or at best to be confined to one class within a school.

Classroom organization

Too little attention has been paid in the past to how teachers cope with introducing new ideas to a class of lively children. The Plowden ideal of individualization — the motivated child learning at his or her own pace — is not easy to achieve in the average primary school. Consequently, workcards have been adopted as a way of allowing children to work individually, while allowing the teacher to attend to particular children who queue at her desk for attention. In practice, this can lead to boredom when a child completes a workcard only to be presented with another (1) or frustration when time is spent waiting for the teacher (3). Individual topic work can also create this dilemma, as lack of close supervision can lead to copying from books and pictures without thought or understanding. Therefore, careful consideration should be given to how the class is organized. All of the contributors describe how they tried to come to terms with this problem in their own classrooms.

The role of computers

Computers raise the challenge of the 'information age', and demand another set of techniques which need to be acquired by teachers and children. Microcomputers can certainly be used to help in classroom organization by fulfilling a 'workcard' function which includes interactive and patient reinforcement. However, their capabilities as information handling devices make it possible to demonstrate how databases are created and so to teach the important lesson that the computer will only retrieve what is put into it, and then only if we frame the questions properly. At best, the computer should take its place as a tool with other learning aids, encouraging logical, sequential thought and the importance of accuracy — valuable adjuncts to information skills. Martin Jackson's account of work in his school concentrates on this creative use of computers as part of topic work.

Books and libraries

Apart from the teacher, books are still the main sources of information. Because they are so familiar, they are often not used as effectively as they might be; book *skills* are often assumed to be acquired by book *use*. We should demonstrate to the children from an early age that 'information books' are (or should be) organized for information retrieval with contents pages, indexes and bibliographies and that clues such as the dates when they were published can help us to assess their usefulness as an information source. This, of course, has implications for the books we select for our schools and how many we throw away as not being not worthy of their place on the school's bookshelves. I know that declining expenditure on books makes throwing away indifferent or outdated books difficult, but their presence is less damaging if children are helped to use them critically.

The organization of library resources in school if often a clue to the way in which we regard information skills. If information retrieval is to be efficient, and seen to have a place in an information skills programme, then the library should be well organized. Middle and top juniors need to be able to identify specific subjects quickly and efficiently, so precise subject codes should be used. For example, children of that age should not have to search through shelves of books on Nature Study to find those on butterflies. They are capable of understanding number codes and coping with subject indexes if we explain how and why this is done or, better still, if they are actively involved in the process of classification and coding. Computing in primary schools is, at its best, challenging the assumptions of children's capabilities and efficient organization of a library is not beyond them either.

Whole school policies

Experience leads me to believe that information skills can be practised early, perhaps from the reception class onwards. Consequently, I see whole school policies as important in ensuring their gradual development. The skills already encountered can be practised and extended, and new ones introduced as children become ready. As yet there is little evidence to show how much can be achieved at various ages and it is possible that much more could be achieved earlier than most of us imagine. One of the benefits that comes from whole school planning is that it helps to give us a better picture of children's capabilities at each stage of the primary school.

If, as this book suggests, information skills can be successfully developed and fostered with infants and juniors, the foundations for successful learning are well laid down for their secondary education and for their future lives.

2

Introducing information skills in the infant school

Until recently, the teaching of information and study skills has been developed mainly at secondary and tertiary levels of education. However, many skills which are necessary in an effective search for and use of information are common to all levels of education. For example, it is difficult to use an alphabetical index without a sound knowledge of alphabetical order. Such a point may seem obvious, but many secondary school children, or even adults, are unable to use indexes competently. They may also experience difficulty in using scanning and questioning techniques to find relevant information quickly from a book, resorting instead to reading laboriously from beginning to end. Because it can be difficult and time consuming to master these skills later in life, it is extremely important to identify and practise them at the earliest possible stage, and, indeed, in the infant classroom. Infants are, of course, taught the alphabet and simple book use in many schools, but Diana Davies' account of her work in the next chapter, shows how this can be integrated into an information skills programme. Her children were learning skills and how to apply them at the same time. In a sense it is not important which materials were used to accomplish this, but I suspect that many teachers will be surprised that some children of this age could begin to use telephone directories or television programme schedules. The strength of her ideas in developing these exercises is, I think, that children were able to see the usefulness of their newly practised skills, and because they had the opportunity to practise them in 'real' situations, their competence rapidly improved.

No one would claim that the skills which infant school children can master are limitless: for example, notetaking is probably an area where the ability develops later. However, I believe the foundations of study and information skills can and should be laid when working with young children. The important factor is an awareness that this can be done, and an effort to build it into the infant school curriculum alongside reading and language development.

2

Introducing information skills in the infant school

Diana Davies

My initial interest in information skills had two sources. One was the growing dissatisfaction I began to feel several years ago with the kinds of reading and writing that children of six and seven were doing, in my top infants class. They wrote their news and good stories, and they read their reading books and books from the class book corner. All this was fairly satisfactory stuff, but I felt they should be using their recently acquired reading skills to find things out, to unlock different kinds of learning.

Why, I wondered, should these children not be able to find things out from books? So I presented them with a collection of books and said, 'Find out something about houses.' They rather hopelessly leafed through the books, but as they hadn't the first idea about how to begin, didn't manage to find out anything much at all. My initial starting point was, of course, too vague and general and I realized that the children needed a much more specific beginning. To help them, I made some question sheets to try to focus their attention on more specific areas. For example, I asked them to find out what kind of houses people lived in a hundred years ago, or what most Elizabethan houses were made of. The results were not much better because, owing to lack of experience, they didn't know which books to look at, or where in the books to look, or how to use an index. So I decided to start a programme of teaching my class to use books from the school library to find out information, asking at first very simple direct questions.

At almost the same time as I was exploring this field with my class, I attended a local in-service course, run by an adviser, on the development of children's reading. This was, among other things, about the very ways of using reading to acquire information which I had been feeling my way towards in the classroom.

Since these joint beginnings I have worked out activities for fostering information skills in all three years of the infant school, trying out many new ideas, some of which have been more successful than others.

Throughout all my experiments in this field I had the support and encouragement of the adviser, both in extending my own work and sharing it with groups of other primary teachers. A junior school colleague and I gave talks to in-service groups about our work on information skills and this collaboration gave me many new ideas. I adapted work with telephone directories which she was doing with her fourth year juniors (ten and eleven year olds) for use by my top infants, aged six and seven. This prompted her in turn to try it with eight and nine year old children in the first and second year of the juniors, on the premise that if infants could do it, so could they.

The school

I teach in an infant school of about two hundred children in an inner city area. The school environment is predominantly one of terraced housing, busy traffic, shops, a few small factories and very little open space. Almost fifty per cent of the children attending the school are Asian, predominantly Sikhs, some of whom have difficulties with English. The classes have over thirty children, some of whom are fluent readers, and some who can read only with great difficulty. At the moment there is one vertically-grouped class of reception and second year children, that is, four, five and six year olds.

The information skills programme

Most of the more advanced information skills work is done in the top year of the infant school, of course, but ground work can be done in the two previous years. I have initiated much of the information skills work in the school when teaching different age groups. Some was tried out by colleagues in the school after initial discussion with me, and with the staff as a whole. Some of the later work for the top year was taken over, adapted and extended by successive teachers.

The following pages give some suggestions for various activities which can be tried out in each year of the infant school. Children, of course, vary in the rate at which they are ready to learn things, and teachers in other schools may find that their children are ready to progress more rapidly. I have arranged the activities by year, but some work, of course, is not confined to a single year. Some categories overlap, some may already be standard practice in your classroom.

Reception year (four and five year olds)

Much that children learn during this year forms the necessary basis for later work, such as the activities and games for learning sounds and the names of the letters of the alphabet.

Pre-dictionary skills
Teachers of reception classes spend a lot of the school year in teaching sounds in various ways; children are taught to recognize letters and know the sound they represent, and also learn, very laboriously, how to write

them. There are many games and many visual aids common to reception classes, such as alphabet-friezes on the wall, pictures of objects beginning with the same letter, tactile letters for the children to feel, sound tables or boxes to hold objects and pictures beginning with a common letter. In my current classroom I have an alphabet train, in which the carriages are pockets made of material, each embroidered with a letter. These pockets hold appropriate pictures and children like to play at putting the cards in the right pocket.

Introducing simple dictionaries

Quite a high proportion of the children in the class, though by no means all, will know the alphabet towards the end of their first year in school, and should begin to see where letters fall in relation to each other. Nearly all the work on the order of letters will have been oral rather than written. Near the end of the first year I begin to look at simple dictionaries, such as Chambers Young Set 1, with small groups of children, showing the guide words and letting them practise how to find words beginning with different letters. I let them browse through the dictionaries on their own too, when they usually compete with each other to find words. It often gets rather noisy; children of four and five seem to be excited by dictionaries, perhaps because they are different from the kind of books they usually look at.

Many children will be ready to attempt simple written work involving the alphabet before the end of the first year. When they begin writing simple sentences on their own, rather than copying under their teacher's writing, the words they need are written in their own personal dictionaries or word books, which are arranged alphabetically. Some children may also be capable of other written work, such as putting missing letters into a sequence, such as a-c-e-g-i-k, and ordering words by the first letter. These children will probably be the better readers in the class.

I tried some written work with a group of three boys and three girls recently, in the summer term of their first year in school. All could read quite well. The girls, two of whom were still not five at the time, were already fluent readers. Previously, the whole class had done a lot of oral work on the letters of the alphabet. I asked the six children to fill in the missing letters on some sheets I had prepared, using the first half of the alphabet, then the second half. I wrote the alphabet out at the top of some of the sheets, and the children with these could fill in the missing letters easily. Some of the group had to refer to the letter frieze on the wall, and one or two found this more difficult. Ben could fill in the letters when he had the alphabet in front of him, but made a mistake when he had to look across the classroom at it.

Then I talked to them about putting words in alphabetical order, according to their first letter, quoting instances from the class register and telephone directories. They knew about telephone directories, but some of them still looked a bit puzzled. When I wrote the words 'apple' and 'zoo' on the board, their brows cleared. 'Oh yes,' they said, 'that's easy. Apple is first.' Next I gave them individual sheets of paper with three words written on each and asked them to place the words in alphabetical order. Tom, then aged five years and four months, a very confident child, said 'Yes, easy', and quickly wrote down the three words in exactly the order I had written them, cat, zebra, apple. Michael aged five and a half, took a long time and fell off his chair twice, but got it right in the end. I thought that Ben, for whom I had written 'dog, sun, ant' had understood, because he got the first word, (which he wrote as 'and') but then after a long pause he wrote 'nus, and' — and I concluded that he hadn't really understood at all. The three girls approached the task differently. Charmaine, nearly five and a half and a very neat, self-contained child, didn't want any help, but after a pause, wrote 'apple, zoo, dog'. Nicola, four years eleven months, sighed a lot. 'Which word are you going to put first?' I asked. 'Well I don't know yet until I think about it', she said. She thought about it, then wrote the words in the correct order. Lorraine, who was the youngest at four years, nine months, looked at her sheet, and wrote the correct answers very quickly and confidently, 'ant, dog, zebra'.

Very young children may therefore, surprise us by being able to order words alphabetically. They find dealing with two words much easier than three, and exercises involving several words are probably better left until a later stage in their school career.

Library skills

By 'library skills' I mean learning to use books from the library, or any other source, to find information. This can involve learning where books are stored in a library, and how to use contents pages and indexes.

One can begin to teach children these skills from the very start of the reception year. When I am reading to a class at the beginning of the autumn term, I point out that I am reading the black squiggly marks on the page, not the pictures, although we can find out a lot of what the book is about from pictures. From time to time I point out the author's name to them. They know that books are made up by real people because my husband, who has written many books for children, comes into school sometimes to read to them. (They do rather tend to think that he makes the whole thing from start to finish though, including the paper!) A class usually wants to know the name of the person 'who did the pictures', as of course the illustrations in a book are very important to a small child. They can also be shown page numbers, where they exist, though unfortunately they are often omitted in books for infants, and learn that the name of a book is known as the 'title'.

I also show them the contents page and index, if there is one, in non-fiction books, but they usually can't begin to use them until they are older.

All this can be shown to the whole class as you are reading books at story time, or whenever you are looking at books with individuals or groups. I also like to send small groups of children to the school library with mothers, or any other helpers, just to browse among the books.

If presented with a smallish selection of books, such as in the class book corner, children can often find books on particular topics, for example, on cats or toys, using the picture on the cover as a guide. When they cannot read very fluently, they can only use illustrations as a way of assessing books. Preety, when asked to choose which book she liked best from a pile she hadn't seen before, chose one with good pictures. She couldn't give any other reason for choosing it apart from the fact that it looked nice.

Middle year (five and six year olds)

Much of the information skills work in this year is a continuation of work begun in the previous year. I have divided it into broad areas, which tend to overlap.

Access skills

By 'access skills', I mean manipulating letters of the alphabet, ordering words by first or subsequent letters, that is, learning skills which are necessary later for finding information from, for example, a telephone directory.

I do try to explain to children why it is useful to know the alphabet and the order of letters. The alphabetical list they know best is the class register and some will know a little about such things as telephone directories.

Most children in their second year can attempt written work on putting in missing letters of the alphabet, a few letters at a time, and can order by the first letter of the alphabet (see Figure 1). Teachers are often surprised at the ease with which second year children can do this kind of task when trying it for the first time, often needing no help at all.

Dictionary skills

Most children will by now have their own word books, or personal dictionaries to use when they write stories, and can this year begin to use simple printed dictionaries properly. As in the reception year, I would introduce dictionaries to a group first, and do group oral activities before trying any written work. For example, I ask them all to try to find the word 'house' in the dictionaries I have given them, or to find two words beginning with 'b'. Children can begin to use dictionaries to find out what words mean,

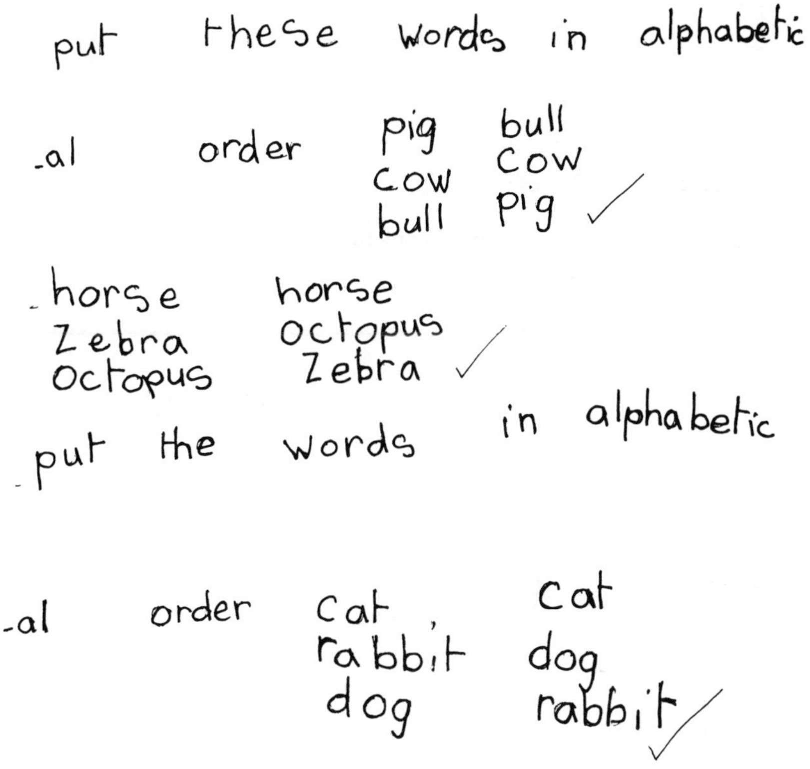

put these words in alphabetic

-al order pig bull
cow cow
bull pig ✓

-horse horse
Zebra octopus ✓
Octopus Zebra

put the words in alphabetic

-al order cat cat
rabbit dog
dog rabbit ✓

Figure 1

and can also use them to check spelling. In the example in Figure 2, Lakhbir was doing an exercise to find out meanings of words, to accustom her to using a dictionary.

Children also enjoy writing down words they find, and even those who are not very good at reading yet can take part, for example, writing down all the words they can see beginning with 'h', perhaps using very simple dictionaries with no definitions, such as Chambers 1.

Library skills
We continue to look at books with children in this year, talking about titles, authors and contents pages. Some good readers may be able to attempt to use an index to find information from a book, probably with some assistance from the class teacher.

Children can also have the organization of the school library explained to them in simple terms. Fiction should be distinguished from nonfiction sections, and any coding which is used should be explained. I took a group

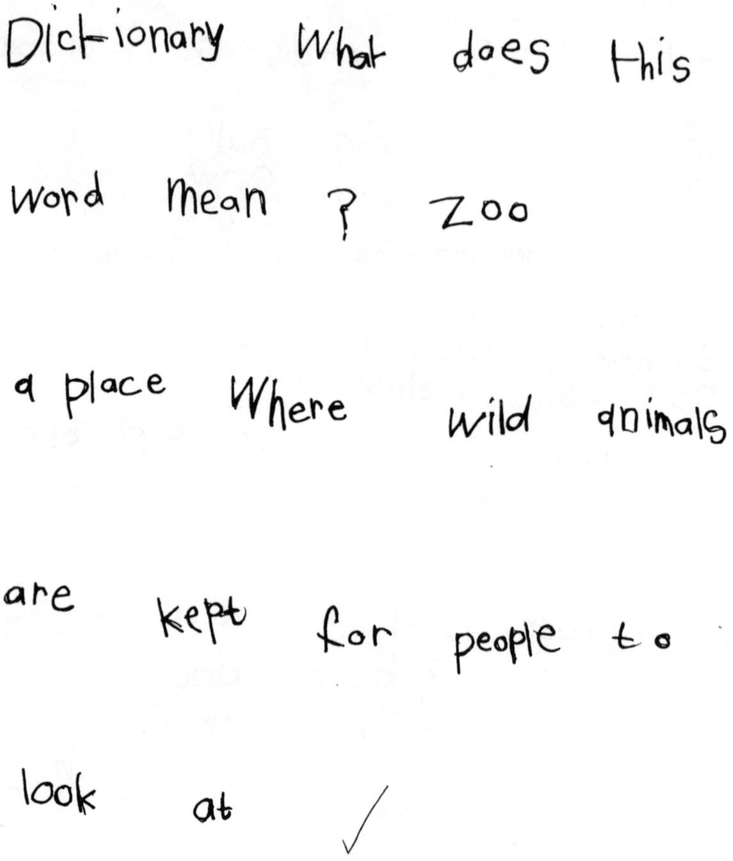

Dictionary   What   does   this

word   mean   ?   Zoo

a place   Where   wild   animals

are   kept   for   people   to

look   at   ✓

Figure 2

of ten second year children into the school library recently and asked them to find books from different sections. Most of these children find reading rather difficult, so I made the tasks very easy, for example, 'Find me a book about birds', and all except one child could find the right kind of book, mostly by looking at the pictures on the cover and inside the book. Some also tried to read a few words. Incidentally, if books are displayed with their spines outwards in the school library, and this is often necessary because of lack of space, young children experience much more difficulty in finding the books they want.

Top year (six and seven year olds)

Access skills
In their last year in the infant school children should be able to understand

much more readily the reasons for learning things such as alphabetical order, and enjoy practising their skill in high speed oral work, going forwards and backwards along the alphabet, finding which letter comes two before 'g' or between 'l' and 'n', thinking of six words beginning with 'b', 'cl', and so on. They are by this time doing sound blends, of course.

The best readers in a top year class can order words by the first, second and third letter, and appreciate the usefulness of this for looking up names in telephone directories. A group of six children, all fluent readers, surprised me the first time I tried 'deep' alphabetical ordering by seeing instantly what I meant them to do. I was halfway through a laborious explanation, when 'Yes, yes,' they said, 'We see how to do it', though Kulwinder made one mistake (see Figure 3). The original order of words is on the left in this example.

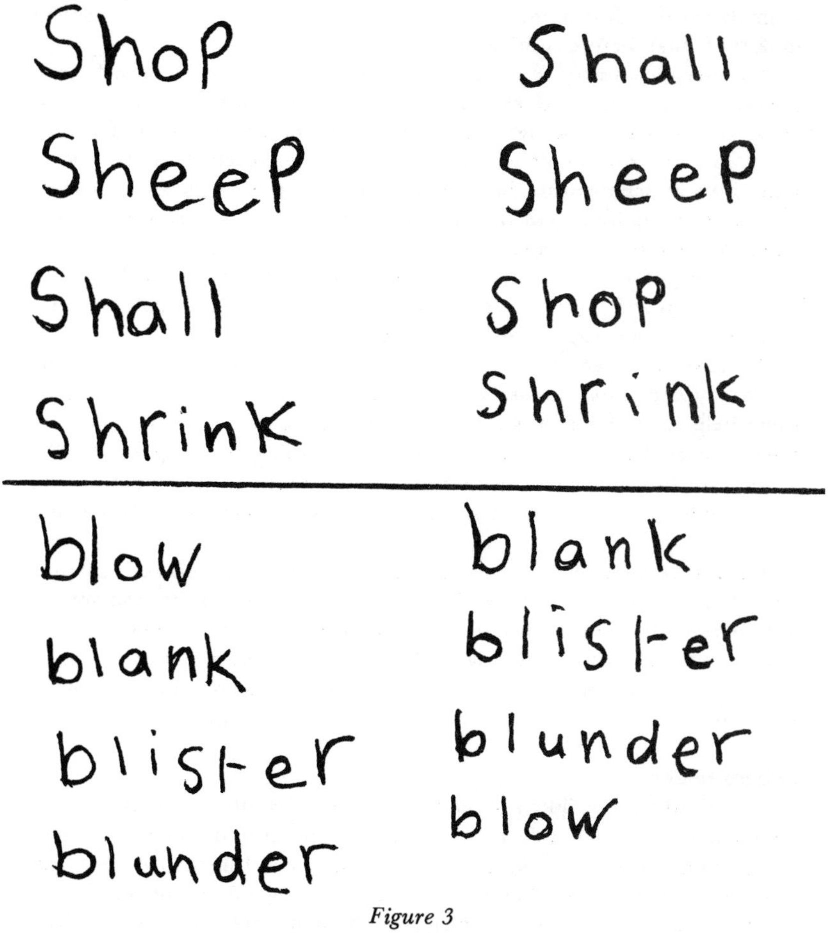

Shop	Shall
Sheep	Sheep
Shall	Shop
Shrink	Shrink
blow	blank
blank	blister
blister	blunder
blunder	blow

Figure 3

Not all the children in this particular class could order words in such a sophisticated way, and some never learnt to do so, even by the end of the school year. At the same time as Kulwinder was ordering words by the third letter, the least advanced readers were finding the right letters to put in spaces in the alphabet, and only learnt to order by the first letter with great difficulty.

Dictionary skills

When children use their own word books in the third year for spelling words, it is all too easy to let them get into the habit of automatically coming to the teacher for any word they need. They should be gently encouraged to be a little more independent. They often have the word they need in their word books anyway, and are surprised and rather shamefaced if this is pointed out; so the first thing they must learn is to look there first, before rushing out to ask.

Another ploy to try is to suggest that they try to write the word themselves, in their word books, and show it to the teacher. After helpless cries of 'but I don't know how!' they sometimes amaze themselves by being able to write simple words on their own. We recently had two poets visiting us at school who did a writing workshop with the two top year classes. The children were not in their usual classrooms, so were parted from their word books, and were horrified at being asked to write without them. The poets and teachers had a busy time giving oral spellings, but both children and teachers were gratified at how much the children could write without the prop of the word book.

A classroom needs to have a good selection of various kinds of dictionaries for children to use in checking spelling, though they may need some help with this at first. I think it is important that they should see their teacher using dictionaries, perhaps her own, to look up words. She should not be afraid to admit that she is occasionally unsure about how to spell words, and it can be reassuring for a class to look up words together with her.

I continue written exercises with dictionaries during this final infants' year. If they don't have to spend too long on written exercises and are not left to flounder with words too difficult for them, children enjoy using their newfound skills in this way. They can find out meanings of words and which words come before and after other words, as in the example in Figure 4.

Library skills

By the third year children should have some idea of the layout of their school library and be able to make an attempt to find a book on a particular topic. The following is an account of work I introduced to a top year class. Again, I started with exercises, using library books, before asking them to try a topic and find information out from books themselves.

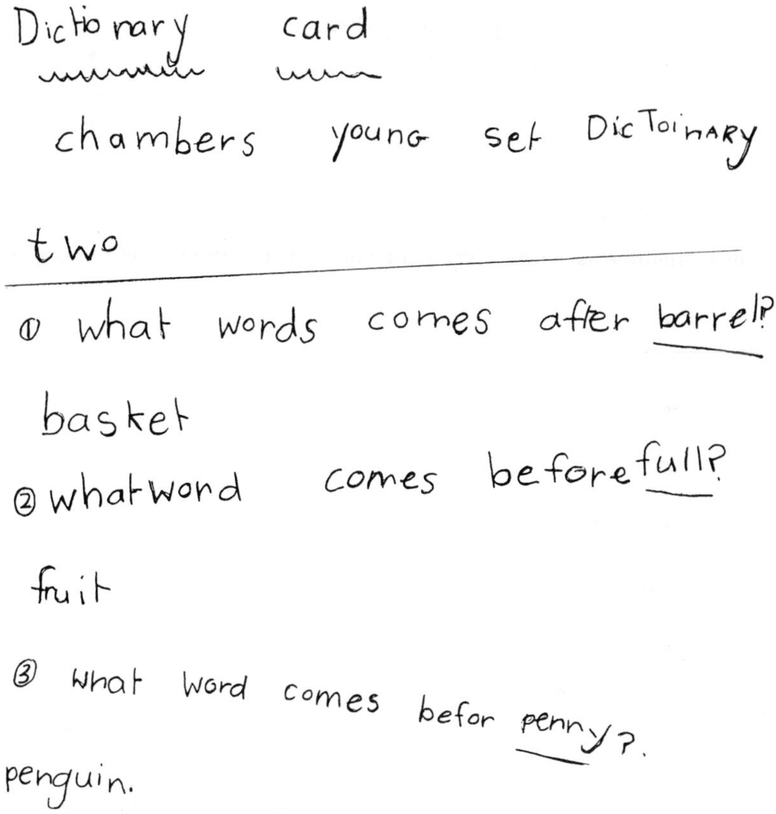

Dictionary   card

chambers   young   set   Dictoinary

two

① what words comes after barrel?

basket

② what word   comes before full?

fruit

③ What word comes before penny?.

penguin.

Figure 4

I began by making some simple workcards, about specific books, asking the children to find out some easily accessible information. I think it is important to start off by asking the children simple, literal questions, building up their confidence by giving them a taste of success right at the beginning. Initially, I also think it wise to use books that they find easy to read, as coping with a difficult text and trying to extract information from it is a lot to ask of a six year old.

Figures 5 and 6 show examples of workcards that I would give a good reader early in the year. The one on Animal Disguises is the more difficult of the two.

The particular good readers with whom I started this work, could do it easily, though they sometimes needed a little help in finding the books. I was interested to see that they all wanted to copy out the question, even though I told them they need not, seeming to need the security it gave them.

I encouraged the children to reproduce the information in their own

Library card

Macdonald Starters - Television

- pink tag

1. P4. What does a television picture look like close up?

2. P9. What are the people doing?

3. Which page tells you how television pictures are sent thousands of miles?

4. P17 Why are there TV cameras in this tunnel?

5. Which is your favourite television programme?

Figure 5

words, rather than copy a chunk out of the book, but they found this difficult, and I think they were only partially successful. I think that the top year in the infant school is probably rather early for children to master this skill, and I would only suggest that they try, not insist upon it. Kulwinder could not understand at first what I wanted her to do and in the end hit on a compromise. 'I have read this page,' she wrote, 'and what it said was . . . ' and then copied it out. I decided to settle for that!

More and more of the class tried these workcards during the school

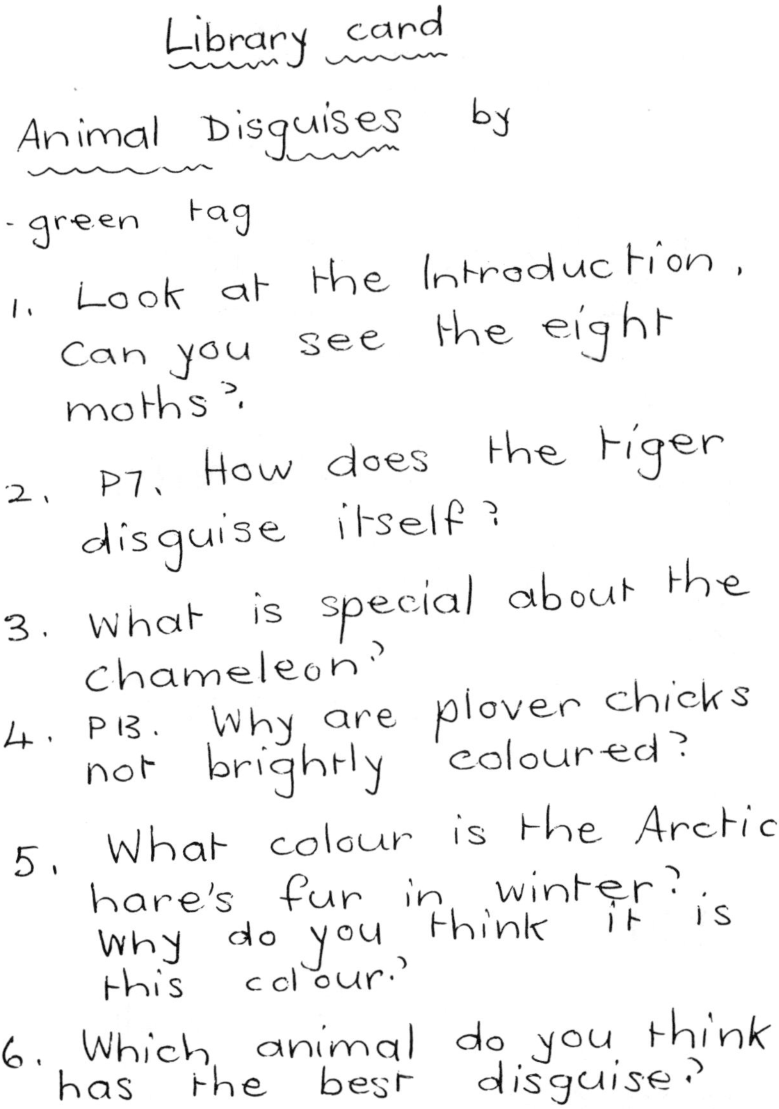

Library card

Animal Disguises by

- green tag

1. Look at the Introduction. Can you see the eight moths?

2. P7. How does the tiger disguise itself?

3. What is special about the chameleon?

4. P13. Why are plover chicks not brightly coloured?

5. What colour is the Arctic hare's fur in winter? Why do you think it is this colour?

6. Which animal do you think has the best disguise?

Figure 6

year, and by the end of it even the very slowest readers managed to do them, though one or two of them did need some help from me in reading the questions and finding the books.

Later in the year I asked some of the children to try making their own question cards. They enjoyed doing this very much and didn't think of it as 'work' at all, though it took some of them a long time to frame questions. They often spent half an hour or so browsing in the library before finding a suitable book, rejecting those without indexes or page numbers. The questions were mostly literal ones, as in the example in Figure 7.

Some of the less able readers wanted to try making their own cards

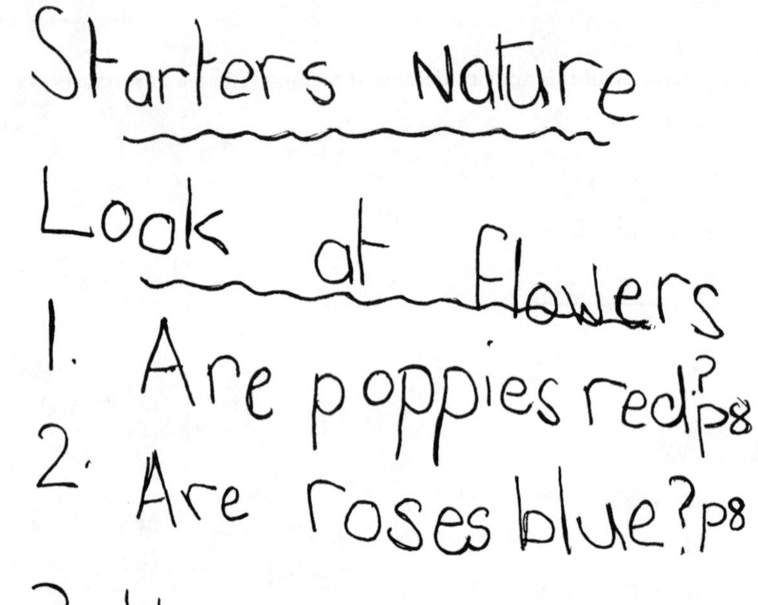

Starters Nature

Look at flowers

1. Are poppies red?p8

2. Are roses blue?p8

3. How do daffodils and tulips Grow p11

4 Where do voets. grow?p13. By Jacaueline.

Figure 7

next. Indeed, making workcards for other children to do became very fashionable in my class. They made library cards, dictionary cards and cloze procedure cards, written in rough first, then in best writing with a pen on a proper workcard. The logical end to all this was, of course, that the children should mark the work which they had set in the first place. I supervised this very closely but they did the marking very carefully and conscientiously, helping other children with difficulties, correcting spelling, and giving stars and comments like 'Good girl'.

I encouraged all this activity because it seemed valuable in several ways:

1) The children were writing for a very clearly defined audience, from whom they experienced very rapid feedback.
2) Devising the workcards involved thorough use of the school library and very close examination of the books in it.
3) Framing the questions was quite a difficult task, and involved a lot of thinking.
4) They enjoyed the process, as it made them feel very adult and responsible, while at the same time they thought of it as fun.

From time to time during the school year the children used the library for finding information on various class topics, and at the end of the year each child, singly, in pairs or groups, produced work for a topic of their own choice, asking themselves:

1) 'What do I already know?'
2) 'What do I want to know?'

They attempted to use library books and books from the public library to find out things they wanted to know, with varying degrees of success. In spite of the work we had done, some still needed quite a lot of assistance, so it would seem that children in the top year of the infants are only just beginning to be able to use books for finding out information.

I must mention here that I did not only point the children towards books as a resource. They often asked people for information and knew that they could glean a lot from pictures, television, radio, magazines and newspapers.

Related work using newspapers and telephone directories

This particular top year class were such avid consumers of information material that I cast about halfway through the year for ways to extend their horizons, and started adapting material a junior school colleague was using with third and fourth years. This involved using advertisements and television programme times in newspapers and the *Radio Times* and *TV Times*. I thought my class would probably find it too difficult to deal with a whole newspaper, so I cut out sections and mounted them on card.

I wasn't at all sure how well they would be able to cope, so I included some easy literal questions, such as 'What time is Laurel and Hardy on?'

My daughter, who was then thirteen, read the cards and thought they would be much too hard for six and seven year olds, but this was not the case. Each year I have tried them with a group of half a dozen children first, explaining to them the different ways of writing time, such as 7.55 p.m. Each year they have fallen on them with great relish, saying 'This is fun'.

Less able readers needed help from me but all enjoyed this sort of thing very much, partly because the cards were different from their usual work, but partly I think because they felt that they were 'real' reading, connected with 'real' things outside school.

I have also used advertisements in newspapers, school dinner menus, and telephone directories, as shown in Figure 8.

I used both ordinary directories and the Yellow Pages. Children found them quite difficult, partly because of the size of print, and partly because of the many abbreviations, such as Rd, and St. I did attempt to use whole directories but abandoned this, as children found them so unwieldy, though we did use the Dialling Code booklet more successfully.

I tried many other kinds of material, such as calendars and lists of Top Ten records, and the children enjoyed them all. You will be able to think of many different sources for yourself.

Classroom organization

It is important to consider classroom organization because we sometimes find it difficult to see how we can fit teaching information skills into a busy school day. I have found that such teaching can often be done casually and informally, at story time for instance in the reception year. When teaching middle and top years, I deliberately include it in my programme of teaching for the day or week.

Reception year

Early information skills work is so much a part of what children learn in the reception year that it is integrated into the normal classwork. Intially, I group children roughly by their assessed readiness to learn to read. Some work is done with the whole class, for example oral work on sounds. Some, for example looking at dictionaries and written work, is done in groups.

Middle year

In this year there would be some class work, for instance on sounds, and some group work. I usually rotate various activities over one day, (see p. 24). The names of the animals were chosen by the groups of children themselves.

Menu card

	FIRST CHOICE	SECOND CHOICE
	APRIL 16th — 30th	
MONDAY	Hot Forend, Pineapple sauce Peas and Carrots. Saute potatoes	Pizza (individual) coleslaw, chips
	Golden sponge, custard	Instant whip, shortbread finger
Cut of Meat or Non Meat	FOREND	CHEESE
TUESDAY	Savoury Mince, Puff Pastry Pieces, Root Veg. Creamed Potatoes	Battered Sausage, Spaghetti, Chips
	Tea Loaf, Squash	Vanilla Slice, Squash
Cut of Meat or Non Meat	CLOD V.P.	SAUSAGE
WEDNESDAY	Roast Pork, Stuffing Green Veg. Roast Potatoes	Fish Fingers, Peas, Chips
	Pineapple Gateaux	Jam & Cream Sponge

1. Which day is there sausage?
2. Which day is there pineapple gateaux?
3. Could you have roast pork and cream sponge on Wednesday?
4. Which day is there pizza?
5. What is your favourite meal?

Figure 8

The children have simple tasks at the beginning of the year, progressing in difficulty. There would probably only be one play activity by the end of the year.

Lions	Horses	Zebras	Dinosaurs
Access skills	Jigsaws	Number	Tracing
Tracing	Access skills	Jigsaws	Number
Number	Tracing	Access skills	Jigsaws
Jigsaws	Number	Tracing	Access skills

Top year

Some work this year would still be done as a class — oral work of various kinds, discussions, and some introduction to new work and ideas. A lot of work would be done in groups, with activities rotated over a week, with the information skills work incorporated into the week's activities. This is an example of a possible week's work for one group. For ease of organization, there would probably be five groups in a class.

Monday	Tuesday	Wednesday	Thursday	Friday
News	Dictionary work	Number	Story	Access skills
Number	Number	Topic	Number	Comprehension work
Measuring	Shapes	Time	Phonic work	Number

Again, the children would have simple tasks at the beginning of the year. A group of six to eight children should try things first, working with the teacher initially, then more independently.

Problems

I have already described some initial problems I encountered, for example my lack of success when asking children to find information without any preliminary experience and without a clear question to answer. This is a brief list of other problems you may encounter

1) Many books currently in infant school libraries are of very doubtful value, either being too difficult, too simple, too out-of-date, or simply falling to pieces. Obviously, a teacher has to work with what is there and library books can only gradually be replaced. Too many information books for infants lack indexes or even page numbers. Books currently being published are, on the whole, of higher quality, but do not always contain much real information, the text being merely a commentary on the pretty pictures. A book which says 'the mother is playing with her kittens', is not much use even to the youngest infant, who can see perfectly well what is going on in the pictures anyway.

2) When working with directories, children sometimes have initial difficulties with abbreviations, but usually only need a brief explanation of how to deal with them. Smallness of print is not so easily overcome and the younger the child the harder they find it to read. Using a ruler to follow the line of print across in a directory may help. I found whole directories too big and heavy to use, but you may find children can cope better with Yellow Pages and the Dialling Code booklet.

3) Some teachers have told me they think young children find it confusing to learn about both names and sounds of letters. Even when teaching a reception class I have not really found this to be so. Many children come into school already knowing the names of letters. Of course, they have to learn the sounds of letters too, but I have not noticed them getting particularly confused about this. In the first year I would put most emphasis on the sound of letters anyway.

4) Dictionary work — care must be taken over this on two counts:
   a) The children should not just look up a work and parrot its meaning without understanding it.
   b) If work is being set by children for others to do you must be careful that it is not too difficult or long, for instance, a list of twenty or so obscure words.

5) Writing information in their own words — this seems to be difficult for young (and not so young) children to do, and I couldn't claim to have been totally successful. I think perhaps it comes with lots of practice and assistance at a much later stage, and when teaching infants one can only lay the foundations of learning such a skill.

6) Finally, there is the difficulty of finding a balance between exercise and 'real' reading for a purpose. There must be a balance and teachers must be aware of the dangers of keeping children on exercises to practise skills without actually using them for any real purpose. Yet I firmly believe that children at this age cannot just be plunged into information skill work with no previous preparation. They must be given the tools they need for informational reading and this is bound to involve doing exercises and practice work with, for example, alphabetical ordering. Children usually enjoy practising skills and can understand some of the reasons for learning them. But they should be moved towards using their skills in a 'real' situation as soon as possible, for example finding books for themselves which answer their questions.

The work I did with newspapers and directories with my top year classes was always regarded by them as real reading, in fact not work at all but 'fun', which is perhaps the aim we should always have in view.

A few years ago I would never have thought that infants were capable of doing the sort of work on information skills which I have seen them do from the age of four onwards. If you try out any of the ideas in this chapter I hope that you too will be pleasantly surprised.

3

Information skills for children with learning difficulties

One problem frequently raised by teachers is that of successfully teaching information skills in a class of mixed abilities. As other chapters suggest, it is possible to go some way in overcoming the problem by careful grouping so that the less able are helped by the other children. However, where more severe learning difficulties occur, it is necessary to ensure that basic skills are mastered successfully before further progress can be made.

Ann Lewis's account of her work with the less able is a valuable contribution to this area. The games she describes can be adopted in any primary classroom to help in strengthening alphabet and dictionary skills.

The development of a good vocabulary is an important foundation for fluency in reading and writing, and the use of dictionaries can play an important part in this. Teachers who took part in this work were satisfied that the skills developed by the games were valuable for reading and writing tasks, and that the pupils became increasingly confident and competent as a result of their participation in the games.

3

Information skills for children with learning difficulties

Ann Lewis

It is a truism that all teachers are teachers of children with special educational needs. One hopes that support for children with a wide range of learning and behavioural difficulties in ordinary schools will increase following the Warnock Report on provision for children with special educational needs (1) and the 1981 Education Act. It has been estimated that in the average primary school class of thirty children, five will have some form of special educational need (1). Most of these children are likely to have learning difficulties, possibly in addition to other special educational needs. In these circumstances, there is a need for teaching of all aspects of the curriculum to include specific provision for these children. This applies as much to the teaching of information skills as to reading, language or mathematics.

Primary schools have recently been criticised for their failure to systematically teach information and study skills (2, 3). However, as Ralph Tabberer has noted, 'At all levels of schooling study skills teaching is already taking place.' (4) It seems that the teaching of information skills has probably also been happening, but in an unsystematic, haphazard manner. While children with average or above average abilities in relevant school tasks may pick up information skills, this is not likely to be the case for children with learning difficulties. These children will not intuitively 'know' how to use an index or a dictionary, but require careful, structured teaching.

A common theme in information skills is the ability to select the relevant piece of information for the purpose in mind from a range of material. This is illustrated at at early level in the use of simple dictionaries. The inability of many children with learning difficulties in primary schools to use simple dictionaries creates a perennial problem for the class teacher. The children ususally begin by being very enthusiastic about writing, but they are continually floored by an inability to write down what they have in mind. Their ideas, even if limited, still exceed their spelling vocabulary. Consequently, the teacher and/or other children are interrupted with requests for 'words'. After a while the child with learning difficulties tends to conclude that it is easier and far less troublesome if he asserts that he has not got anything about which to write. The work described here was an attempt to provide a programme for children with learning difficulties which would overcome these problems. The activities have been used with less able six and seven year olds in a first school, and with eight to eleven year olds in a school for children with moderate learning difficulties. It is felt that they are appropriate for children with learning difficulties throughout the primary age range.

The use and function of dictionaries

It was decided that before suitable programmes could be planned and carried out, the teachers involved would attempt to determine the types of strategies and concepts which the children employed when trying to find a word which they wanted to write. The decision to make this the first step was influenced by the work of various researchers who have analysed children's perceptions of print and have found that children's concepts of 'word', 'sentence' and 'letter', for example, were very different from those held by adults (5, 6). A number of interesting points emerged from observations and discussions with these children concerning the nature of dictionaries.

1 Reliance on picture cues

Most of the children were still heavily reliant on using the pictures in early word books and dictionaries to locate chosen words. Only the more confident seven year olds, and none of the other children, were prepared to tackle the task of finding a word in a non-illustrated dictionary (and eventually succeeded in locating the desired word!). The children were at different stages in their use of the picture cue. Many of the children over-relied on the picture cue and therefore made many errors; 'ant' for 'spider', 'children' for 'boy', for example. Some children were more sophisticated in their use of the picture cues. For example, several children rejected specific words, having realised that although the picture fitted, the initial letter of the given word was inappropriate. Hence the rejection of 'fairy' for 'queen' and 'doll' for 'puppet'. One girl, when asked to find 'puppet' in the word book, questioned the teacher at length about what a puppet was and, finally satisfied, said, 'O, one of them things with strings'. However, interestingly, the picture cue for puppet was of a hand puppet not a marionette and lacked strings! In spite of this the girl correctly identified the word 'puppet'. She clearly understood that the initial letter, being correct, was of more significance than the details of the picture cue.

2 Rote knowledge of the alphabet

Most of the children said the alphabet by rote without using any sort of cue card, and some of them were particularly proud that they could even recite the alphabet with their eyes shut! However, none of the children could make the connection between knowledge of the alphabet and the use of a word book or dictionary. Many children, when prompted, realised that 'a' and 'b' words came near the beginning of the book, and some could guess at letters in the middle or end of the alphabet but they could not apply this information to the use of a word book. A boy who was closest to this realisation wanted a strip of card with the alphabet written out in sequence to help him to find where the 'q' for queen was, and therefore whereabouts to start looking in the word book. Surprisingly few word books or simple dictionaries used at this level do seem to incorporate such alphabet strips.

3   The significance of meaningful words

A third interesting observation from work with these children was that a word needed to have meaning for them before they would even attempt to look it up, for example, the girl who wanted to clarify what a puppet was before she looked up the word. This was not a problem when the word books were used to help writing devised by the children, but only when they were given words in isolation to look up by the teacher. This illustrates the importance of using word books and dictionaries only as part of an activity which has meaning for the child and not as an exercise.

4   Page by page searching

All the children approached the task of finding a desired word in the word book or dictionary in the same manner, beginning at page one and patiently turning page by page until they came to it. When asked how they could find the word more quickly the most frequent reply was 'Turn the pages faster'! One child said, 'Start at the back'. He had some idea that this might be quicker but he lacked any guide or rule as to when this strategy might apply. This seemed to be linked to the children's inability to apply their rote knowledge of the alphabet.

More generally it seemed to be typical of the children's 'search' strategies in a relatively abstract context. When they were given a number of different tasks which involved searching for something the same step by step looking from the beginning generally occurred. The exceptions were in the most concrete and, for them, meaningful context. For example, when asked where the school head might be found, the children first suggested 'her room', then, did not suggest looking in class 1, class 2, class 3 . . ., but listed probable places based on their knowledge of the school organization and timetable. Similarly, asked to locate a jar of blue paint in the classroom, when it was not in its usual place, both groups of children suggested a range of probable places. They did not begin to look in all the cupboards round the room in sequence. However, given less meaningful and far more abstract tasks, for example to find a five of hearts in a pack of cards spread face up on the table, or to find a picture of a kettle in a mail order catalogue, the children reverted to going through the cards or catalogue pages one by one.

5   Dictionaries used as word books

All the children considered dictionaries as synonymous with word books and their sole function to be as a source of correct spellings. They had not realised that a dictionary is also a source for word meanings. This finding has been noted in a number of research projects investigating early reading and writing (7). It reflects how rarely dictionaries are used to identify word meanings at this stage and in the classroom teachers themselves usually only use dictionaries to check spellings. When the children were asked, 'What is the difference between a word book and a dictionary?' they were totally baffled. When they were given two different word books and a dictionary, or vice versa, they could not identify the odd one out or work out the distinction between the two types of books. It was felt to be important that children were introduced to the dictionary as a source of word meanings early in their attempts at literacy. This enables children to check the correct written form for a given usage when the words have the same sound (e.g. sow/sew, no/know). It also helps children to learn that words whose meaning is unclear can be checked in the dictionary, and that this can be a source of interest in itself.

6   Preference for asking another child or the teacher for an unknown word

When confronted with wanting to write a word which they did not know how to spell, virtually all the children would ask another child or the teacher to write the word for them. This was the first method which they used. None of the children said that they would guess the word and none said that they would initially look it up, whether on wall charts, in their personal word books or in a class word book or dictionary. This lack of confidence and avoidance of word books or dictionaries is clearly at the root of the organizational problems which arise when free writing activities are carried out with children with learning difficulties.

7   Confusion concerning upper/lower case print and names/sounds of letters

Most of the children associated upper case letters with letter names and lower case letters with letter sounds. This exacerbated certain problems for their use of word books and dictionaries. This confusion may be heightened by children being introduced, at pre-school level, to ABC books which use only single upper case letters whereas early picture dictionaries use initial letters written in lower case print. Difficulties also arise for children with learning difficulties through teachers' use of the ambiguous term 'small letters' (meaning lower case). When children with learning difficulties were explicitly taught to use and understand the terms 'upper case' and 'lower case', they quickly picked this up and avoided such confusion.

Common areas of difficulty

This observation and discussion concerning the use of word books and dictionaries with children with learning difficulties revealed two main hurdles for them. The first was the transition from using simple picture 'dictionaries' to applying knowledge of alphabetical sequence in the use of non-illustrated dictionaries. It is interesting that this difficulty has been acknowledged by an American publisher who produces a 'pictionary' to help bridge this stage (8). The second hurdle was in the transition from word books to dictionaries with the accompanying emphasis on the dictionary as a source of meanings. Therefore a programme of activities was devised specifically to take the children through these two particularly difficult stages. It did not extend to the later stages of dictionary skills involving, for example, the use of guide words, pronunciation symbols and accents or conventions denoting parts of speech and word origins.

Maximizing the classroom environment

The specific activities designed to help develop the use of simple dictionaries were planned to go alongside normal classroom practices. There was considerable discussion among the teachers involved about how they could use the classroom environment to stimulate the effective and efficient use of dictionaries. The suggestions included:

1 Ensure that *classroom lists* are in alphabetical order e.g. colour words, weather words.
2 Draw children's attention to the alphabetical order of names in *school registers*.
3 Occasionally *line children up* in alphabetical order when going into assembly, etc.
4 Have several fixed *alphabet strips* around the room, some in reverse alphabetical order.
5 Put *a border of letters in alphabetical sequence* on some notices.
6 When doing topic work include *key words written in alphabetical order* on an appropriate display, for example, 'house' words written on a very tall chimney in a picture of a house, and 'canal' words written on a barge. These could be made on separate pieces of card so as to slide in and out of the picture or

model. Individuals or small groups of children could make an appropriate model for their own key words.

7 When teaching a particular project include a wall chart of *key words and their meanings*.

8 Make *language master cards* of commonly needed words and store in clearly labelled wall pockets in alphabetical order. In practice this gave rise to much valuable sorting work both within and between letter groupings.

9 Make short *cassette tapes* to go with the personal word books of the least able children. (In practice this was only successful where the total number of words included was fairly small, i.e. 25 or less.)

10 Check to see if there is an appropriate word sorting or alphabet programme for the school's particular *micro-computer* and whether or not it will add anything new to existing activities.

11 Encourage children to *glance down the beginning of classroom lists*, e.g. when looking for a colour word. Much early reading material concentrates on teaching reading from left to right, but it is the quick top-bottom scanning which is needed in using word books and dictionaries effectively.

12 Make even the least able child a *personal dictionary* rather than word book from the start. The child gives the teacher the word and definition (initially very simply, e.g. Wayne — my brother) and the teacher writes it in the child's personal dictionary. In this way children learn from the beginning the prime dual functions (spelling and word meaning) of a dictionary.

Aims of the programme

The specific programme to develop dictionary skills for children with learning difficulties was planned with five aims in mind:

1 The activities should be fun. The message which we hoped to convey was that playing with letters and words using dictionaries is enjoyable, not onerous.

2 The activities should be meaningful, that is, we wanted the children to see the connection between the game and the use of a dictionary as an aid to their desire to communicate. These activities were a means to an end, not an end in themselves.

3 Wherever possible, the games should be personalized.

4 The presentation of the activities within the classroom organisation should permit them to be self-chosen by children as much as possible.

5 The activities should involve maximum active participation from children. Copying from workcards, which was criticised in the recent HMI survey of first schools, (9) had no place in the programme.

The programme was divided into four stages:

Stage I: Alphabet games
Stage II: Word finding and sorting, based on first letter sound only
Stage III: Word finding and sorting based on first two or three letter sounds
Stage IV: Word meaning games

Stage Ia   Alphabet games based on finding letters within an alphabetical sequence (alphabet recognition)

Note that games involving recognition preceded recall games as the former involves a simpler skill. It is easier for a child to recognise 'b' or 'bird' from a group of letters or words than it is for the child to recall the letter or word entirely from memory without any visual prompts.

Game 1   Name Bingo (individual)
The child has an alphabet strip and separate card pieces with the letters of his or her name written on them. Include upper and lower case letters for initial letters of the child's name, as shown in Figure 1. The child covers the letters on the strip with those from his or her name. Begin this activity as an untimed game, and add the time element later to increase

Figure 1

fluency. Keep a record of times for each child, and aim for 2—3 seconds per letter. When proficient with their own name, the child 'swops names' with another child.

Variation: As above but use 2 half alphabet strips, with the second half of the alphabet written backwards. The aim of the variation is to introduce the child as early as possible to the advantages of going backwards through the alphabet to find a specific letter.

Game 2   Alphabet Bingo (individual)
Use an alphabet strip as for game 1, but divide the strip into two, three or four sections as appropriate for the child, with appropriate single letter cards. Initially untimed and using only part of alphabet, when the child can match letters for part of the alphabet with ease, build up to the whole alphabet and add timed element. Keep a record of the times. Aim for the whole alphabet to be matched in 1—1½ minutes. (Note these times are suggestions only, check their suitability by getting several competent children in the class to do the game and use their average time as the aim for the class.)

Game 3   Bulldog Game (pairs)
One child has a large alphabet strip facing him or her, a partner sits opposite and can see only blank squares. The first child puts a bulldog clip (or a paper clip or plasticine blob) on a chosen letter. The second child guesses which letter it is. Initially he may need his own model alphabet strip as a cue and to give a group of letters rather than a single letter. In practice this game proved to be far more difficult than originally envisaged, as it necessitated the 'guesser' having some notion of the alphabet in reverse (see Figure 2).

Stage 1b   Alphabet games based on sorting single letters into alphabetical sequence (alphabetical recall)

Game 4   Alphabet Snake (individual/pairs)
The teacher writes the alphabet on a long strip of paper or card, then cuts it up into separate letters using a variety of cutting patterns. The child then remakes the snake. Initially, the child may need a model alphabet strip (see Figure 3).

Game 5   Hands (whole class/large group)
The children have large individual letters written on the backs of their hands (this requires 13 to 26 children depending on whether children have letters written on both hands or on only one). The children then have to sort themselves into alphabetical order.

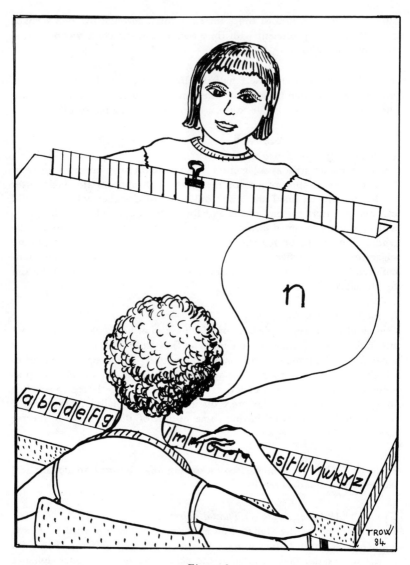

Figure 2

Game 6   *Alphabet Cubes (individual)*

Groups of 4, 5, or 6 cubes are used. The teacher threads them on to thick wire and writes the alphabet sequence on each side. Each side should match up simultaneously (see Figure 4).

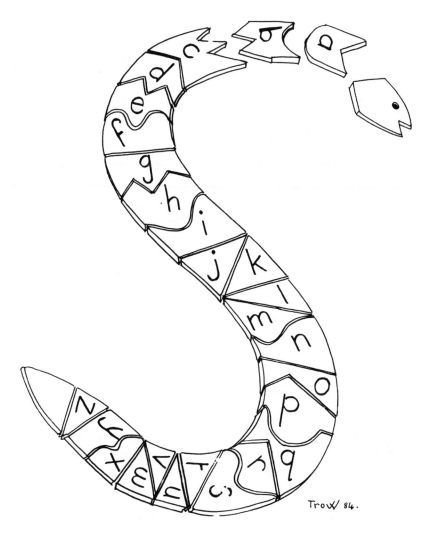

Figure 3

Game 7   Memory Game (group)
The teacher puts out a group of objects, each of which begins with a different letter, in alphabetical sequence, e.g. models (or pictures) of; an apple, a box, a cat, a dog and an envelope. The teacher then hides them (as in 'Kim's game') and children try to recall — in alphabetical sequence — the original objects.

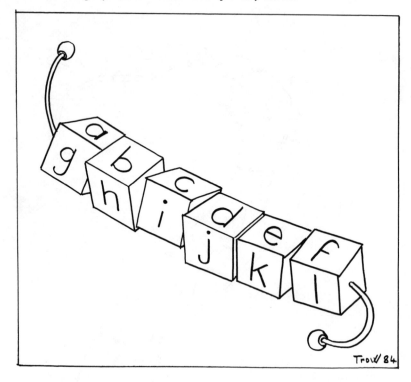

Figure 4

Game 8   Snakes (whole class/large group)
Each child has a letter pinned to his or her back, the spare children (give
two successive letters to one or more children as required if there are no
'spares') collect up the other children in alphabetical order to form a long
snake (see Figure 5). This can be varied by having several children 'collect
up' beginning at different points in the alphabet — the least able children
being given 'a'.

Stage IIa   Word finding, using first letter sound only

Game 9   Word Bingo (group)
Use cards with words written in alphabetical order, preferably words
relevant to the class. The cards are distributed as for standard bingo, the
caller gives a word, and the children who have it on their card cover it up.
Each card contains words in alphabetical order. Initially use groups of words
from one section of the alphabet only on each card (e.g. a-g, e-j, h-o, m-t,
r-y) and only one word beginning with each letter within each group. Later
in Stage III — include several words from each letter group.

Figure 5

Stage IIb   Word sorting, using first letter sound only

Game 10   Collectors (whole class)
The class is divided into groups of 4 to 5 children, and each group is given part of the alphabet and a sheet of newspaper. Words are cut out and given to the appropriate group, who glue the words on to individual sheets to

make a word bank. Initially all the words beginning with the same letter are glued on to one sheet in random order. As children get more proficient, (a) arrange the words within the letter group in alphabetical order, then glue them on, and (b) let the children take it in turns to give or write definitions alongside as many words as possible.

Stage III   Word sorting by first, second and third letters

Game 11   Class Dictionary (whole class)
The children work in pairs, and write 1, 2 or 3 words on separate pieces of paper for a class dictionary (preferably with definitions). The teacher collects them in and redistributes them, having assigned individual letters of the alphabet to children (give popular letters to a pair or small group of children). The children then glue the words in correct alphabetical sequence on individual pages. This can be done for general use, or a specific topic, made up as a zigzag book, wallcharts or a standard book.

Game 12   Codes (whole class/group/pairs)
The children decode and then write their own coded messages using a standard dictionary commonly used by the class. Words are coded by their location in the dictionary; the first number indicates its page number, the second number the column, and the third number its position in the column, e.g. 13.2.5. If done in groups, the level of dictionary can be varied to suit abilities of children.

Game 13   Streets (whole class/group)
The children collect street names, ideally by walking around the local area, then collate them into alphabetical order.
Variation: as above, but collecting car number plates, decide whether the end letters of new cars or the 2/3 letter group is to be the basis for alphabetical sequence.

Stage IV   Word meaning games

Note that Games 10 and 11 can be played as word meaning games. Ideally simple word meaning games should be introduced at the same time as word finding games.

Game 14   Call My Bluff (whole class/group)
As in the TV panel game, three children read out definitions of one word, and the rest guess which is the correct definition (there may be more than one). A checker looks up the word in the dictionary to determine the correct answer. Note that this may be played at a range of levels.

Many variations of the popular classroom activity in which the teacher calls out a word and children have a race to see who can locate the word and definition first, can also be played at this stage.

Monitoring progress

No attempt was made to record the games in which children had participated, as it was felt that the games were a means to an end. Instead, records were kept on the children's progress through a number of key skills. (Note that the skills do not necessarily form a linear progression.)

Target skills of the programme (*denotes key skills)

* 1 Understands that a word is a unit of language (for example, when the child is asked for a word he does not say 's' or 'I like semolina'.
  2 States the beginning sound of a word.
  3 States the sequence of sounds following the first letter sound.
  4 Associates all single letter sounds with their printed symbols.
* 5 Locates correct page in own word book for the teacher to write desired word.
  6 Recognises required word on a given page of word book or dictionary.
  7 Identifies a letter as being at the beginning, middle or end of the alphabet.
  8 Identifies a letter as being in front of or behind a given letter.
  9 Given a single letter and a target letter, knows whether to go backwards or forwards.
 10 Finds commonly used words in a simple dictionary.
* 11 Finds correct letter section of a dictionary efficiently, i.e. not by automatically looking a- b- c.
* 12 Uses dictionary as a source of spelling, freely and accurately in his or her own writing.
 13 Recognises the correct usage of the word for which he or she is looking e.g. sew/sow/so.
* 14 Uses dictionary efficiently to find word meanings in his or her own work.

Organization

In organizational terms it was found that the most useful ways in which to use the games were either as a 'spare time' activity when other activities had been completed and there was a short period before the end of the session, or as activities included in a 'free choice' afternoon. In addition, on many occasions helpers in the school (a parent, a student, a pupil from a neighbouring comprehensive school and young people on a youth opportunity scheme) used the games with a small group of children. Occasionally, teachers held a 'words afternoon' when a mixture of these and other class and group games were utilized.

Conclusion

The games described above have been played successfully with a range of children with learning difficulties. 'Successfully' here encompasses:

1 The children were enthusiastic about the games and enjoyed playing them. They often chose to do so independently of an adult.
2 The games 'worked' in that the children understood how to play them and followed the rules correctly.
3 The teachers were readily able to incorporate the games into the classroom organization. However it was found that introducing and explaining the games to the children took longer than originally envisaged.
4 The children improved markedly at the games and therefore appeared to be learning the salient features. Thus many of the original aims of the programme were accomplished.

In the longer term the effectiveness of these games lies not in their usefulness in keeping children apparently happy and busy, but in whether or not the skills employed transfer to writing tasks and, specifically, the use of simple dictionaries. The impressions of the teachers involved were that this did indeed appear to be happening. They concluded that the games were very useful, within the context of a broader language and literacy programme, in promoting the acquisition of information skills for children with learning difficulties.

4

Information skills through project work

Project work can be a vehicle for many skills in the classroom: reading and language development, group discussion and information skills. It is often criticised for consisting of copying from books, relying on commercial workcards, and so on. This reveals the failure to plan the topic effectively, and means that the possible benefits are unrecognized. They need to be fostered by careful forward planning.

At its best, topic work provides an opportunity for children to acquire and practise the skills of gathering and evaluating information from a variety of sources. The critical use of books and resource materials, letter-writing, reading effectively and presentation of data are examples of skills which can be learnt in a way which directly relates to the work in hand. One important aspect which Wendy Bloom emphasises is the ability to *plan* work, and she describes how the project was planned at each stage of its development in a way that helped children become organizers of their own time and learning. Planning is important too for the teacher.

Classroom organization must be effectively managed so that all the children can benefit from working either individually or in groups. Perhaps, most difficult of all, there is the problem of assessing whether children are in fact developing skills and learning from the topic work. As Wendy Bloom points out, there is a tendency to judge success or failure by the amount of written work produced at the end of a project, but learning can be expressed in other ways — thoughtful contributions to group discussions, a new confidence in handling books, or producing a model which demonstrates understanding and interest in the subject investigated. To quote the author, there is a need 'to balance process and product'.

4

Information skills through project work

Wendy Bloom

Like most teachers, I wanted the children in my class to become more independent in their learning. To become more independent they obviously needed to acquire information skills. These skills needed to be learnt, but I am convinced that real learning only happens for children in a context that has meaning and purpose for them and *not* through drills and exercises.

Working on a project seemed to be the ideal situation for developing information skills. This, then, is a description and discussion of a project about stone and iron age people done with a class of eight to nine year olds in a multicultural school, lasting about one month.

The information skills I wanted to work on with the children through this project were:

1) skimming, scanning and reading closely — being able to see the need for each approach and being able to switch from one to the other.
2) using index and contents pages;
3) starting to look critically at books;
4) making notes;
5) planning questions, ways of working and the eventual form of presentation of information gathered.

I also wanted to have opportunities for different kinds of talk, including planning and discussion of work in small groups, as well as reporting back in more formal terms to the whole class.

In addition, some of the children who were becoming bilingual needed practice in the written forms of the past tense (for which I provided cloze texts). They also needed practice in formulating written and verbal questions, so I planned to meet this need in the project.

I was aware that a good deal of criticism had been aimed at topic work. Children were not getting involved in any prolonged reading or comparing sources, but were just collecting snippets of information. Sometimes they had no real purpose to their investigations and copied out whole chunks from books. Some projects consisted mainly of pupils following work-cards made up by the teacher. Often children ended up with some kind of folder to take home. It seemed sometimes that only the end product mattered — not the actual processes of learning.

Choice and origin of topic

In my school we had agreed upon an overall outline for history and this topic came out of that outline. There were other times when classes chose topics to do with current or environmental themes. Within the class, individual children sometimes chose their own topic.

It is interesting to see the way that different kinds of topics will demand the use of different materials and different kinds of language. A neighbourhood project, for instance, provides a good contrast to a history project. Children can even plan and work in a different way.

However the topic arises, I think that planning and working should be negotiated between teacher and children. Each time that children plan their work, try to use information skills and try to evaluate what they have done, they are acquiring and developing skills with far-reaching applications.

Order of work

I had planned the project to go forward in the following way. At the first session I explained the order to the children.

1) Introduction of topic;
2) Explanation for selecting the subject of stone and iron age people — what we could do with the results of the children's work;
3) Deciding on the different aspects of the people's lives that we could find out about, dividing up the area of enquiry and forming groups;
4) Forward planning in groups — deciding how the project would go forward;
5) Working through the project — monitoring progress and problems (the children *and* I would do this, but in different ways);
6) Holding whole class sessions in reading development;
7) Presentation of work;
8) Evaluation.

1)   Introduction of topic

In the first two sessions the children and I talked about what they already knew or had heard of stone and iron-age times. This included anecdotes about films, television programmes, books and comics. Anecdotal learning has a big part to play in the learning of younger children. We, as adults, learn a lot in this way, too. Think of a formal lecture with points suddenly illuminated by an anecdote! This case study, too, has its roots in anecdote. Arising from our discussion I noted down on the board a preliminary list of things that we might find out about.

During these sessions I led the talk round to some discussion of primary and secondary sources in history. We talked about how difficult it is to be sure what life was really like before events were written down. Before this project, we had been to a local museum and seen and handled fossils. For this project we borrowed flint and iron weapons and tools. These were our only primary sources. Our secondary sources were our books and posters. I tried to explain that these were historians' and archaeologists' interpretations of the evidence. I think that history is a very difficult subject for primary school children in many ways. At the beginning of the year we had spent some time on their own and some of their family histories and talked about diaries. I suppose what I was really trying to do was to help the children realize (perhaps later) that history is an interpretation of past events, not cold facts — an important concept for their future studies of world history.

2)   Explanation of choice of subject and planning for presentation

The reason why we were following this particular topic was straightforward. We were, as a school, following a chronological approach to history at that time. The class had begun the year by looking at the beginning of evolution.

I suggested that to give their enquiry and efforts more purpose, the children should present their results not only to others in the same class but also to the other classes in the same year group. Other purposes that might have been suggested are: an assembly, a corridor display, a presentation for younger children or a display at the local library.

The children suggested several ways of presenting the information. They were: a tape, a tape plus booklet for listening and reading, a large wall poster, a plasticine model with explanatory labels, simulated artefacts with labels, and the usual illustrated folder. We discussed quite briefly what they would have to aim for in each type of presentation. These points were brought out again with individual groups as they began planning their work.

I think it is very important for children to have the mode of presentation in mind from the outset. It is a form of long-term planning and gives an added dimension to the collection and collation of information. While children are reading books and studying posters they must be considering how to interpret, arrange and edit in order to shape their information to suit their final presentation. They must remember their 'consumers' and their likely level of understanding.

3)   Dividing up the area of enquiry and forming groups

From our initial talk about stone and iron age times and from the children's first look at the collection of artefacts, posters and books which we had borrowed from the local museum, we decided on our areas of enquiry.

We were to look at: food, weapons and tools, clothes, shelter, groups, animals, hunting and gathering and burials.

At this point I introduced the idea of making a 'planning matrix', the outline of which I had already drawn on the board (see Figure 1). This was a demonstration using the same outline as the groups used later.

I filled in some 'boxes' with possible questions from the children and we plotted these against possible sources of information also suggested by the children. These possible sources were: books in school; encyclopaedias; public library books; posters; newspapers; magazines and comics; television and radio programmes; film loops; museum objects and letters of enquiry.

Groups

I had decided that the class should work in small groups for the project, as they did with much of their other work. There were three main reasons for this decision: a) the varied use of language that can come from small group work within a whole class setting; b) the effectiveness of this way of organizing learning; c) the increased opportunity for social contact and development.

We negotiated the formation of groups in twos, threes and fours. These were mainly 'friendship' groups but other considerations had to be taken into account. Children with reading or learning difficulties needed to be with someone who would be sympathetic while not 'taking them over'.

With one or two of these children I had to arrange a group prior to the session, while I was confident that others would find a suitable group. For children becoming bilingual it was important that they were in a group with at least one member who would present them with a good model of spoken and written English.

4) Forward planning in groups

The groups chose their topic from the areas we had decided upon and listed. To make this clear, one group drew up a wall chart to show the members of each group, and which topic they were investigating.

Iron and stone age people   Class 1/4

Group	Topic
1 Joanne, Sukjinder, Parminder, Elaine	Food
2 Balraj, David, Jonathan, Jaskinder	Hunting and gathering

I asked each group to begin by filling out a blank matrix, like the one in Figure 1, plotting specific questions against possible sources of information.

Where to find out from									
What to find out	books in school	encyclo-paedias	public library books	posters	newspapers	magazines comics	TV/radio	Film loops	museum objects	writing a letter
How did the stone age people cook their food?	✓	✓	✓	✓				✓		
What weapons did they use for hunting?	✓	✓	✓	✓			✓		✓	

Figure 1   A planning matrix

This could be added to or changed as they went on. Items were checked off as they were completed and each member of the group had a referral point when deciding what needed to be done next. Such a planning tool is important, because:

a) It encourages the children to pre-plan an investigation, and to revise and extend their original thoughts.
b) Deciding on specific questions within a broad area is a valuable thinking process. When children have a particular question in mind they will look for the relevant information in a more organized way — they will *need* to skim, scan, read closely, and to consult an index and contents.
c) Any form of planning future actions is important for children if they are to become independent in their learning. Too often opportunities for planning reside with the teacher.
d) By actually plotting questions against sources in a concrete way on a number of occasions the pupils should gradually make this way of working part of their thinking and habitually become better planners.

5) Working through the project — monitoring progress and problems

Each group was asked to keep up a routine of noting down their progress and any problems. The group chose a scribe for this purpose who usually, but not always, became the group leader. (The need for fluent and legible writing was reinforced here.) Session notes were dated and each group could choose either to state what they would do or to summarize what they had done. This practice generated a more thoughtful and systematic way of proceeding, and provided a point of reference when we talked together.

The scribe was responsible for starting sessions by reading out to the group notes from the preceding session so that they could more easily resume work. This procedure, as well as encouraging discussion and short term planning, was meant to be a model for future individual investigative work. Again I was hoping that this process would become habitual.

The notes were not elaborate and would look something like this:

Date	
Bill	drew spear ⟶ not big enough ⟶ will enlarge
me	looked at *From cavemen to Vikings* for picture of axe ⟶
	to small ⟶ will use poster
Steve	wrote label for spear in notebook ⟶ OK ⟶ will
	copy out

Within the groups, individuals were encouraged to share out tasks and to avoid duplicating information. At this stage, many of the pupils could make quite good attempts at taking notes and further help was given in this (described later in the chapter). I tried to make sure that the children used the notes and not the original source when working on the final presentation, only referring back if queries arose. I explained to the children in simple terms that this method of reading, pausing and thinking about what they had read, then changing it into their own language as they wrote or said it, gave them a good chance of fixing the knowledge in their memory and being able to recall it easily.

During the course of the project, we had interim progress reports from the groups to the whole class. These were kept as brief and businesslike as possible, and usually took place at the end of sessions. We would move tables and sit round in a circle to do this. I kept in touch with each group's progress mainly by informal talking. I had to make sure to keep in regular touch with the 'quieter' groups, who only occasionally asked for my help, as well as the more vociferous groups. Twice during the project I took time to consider all the results to date and left each group with written notes of enquiry and encouragement, to which they responded. By doing this I could think carefully about each group's progress and how they were responding to this way of working. Written comment has permanence as a point of reference, it assumes more importance and is appreciated by children as a considered response to their efforts.

6)   Whole class sessions in reading development

As the work was in progress we consciously made time to practise some reading activities. This was in addition to help given to groups and individuals while they were working on their projects. As pupils came to grapple with books they could see the sense of using 'short cuts' to make themselves more efficient.

We played 'games' with the class dictionaries (everyone must have a copy) to develop quick recall of alphabetical order and thinking about alternative words. These sessions were short and lighthearted. Each time we did this I reminded the children about the index in books, thus linking the practice to further logical application.

We made use of the only textbook which everyone had a copy of, *From Cavemen to Vikings* (1). We practised skimming and scanning, using the index and contents as well as the text to reinforce their purpose and use. This again was treated like a game with competition to be amongst the first ten to locate information or a particular word. We joined together as a class to review the particular book each pupil was using at a given time. We agreed to consider the books under the following headings:

> *Title*
> *Author*

Publisher
Date of publication
Contents and index   (yes or no)
Layout   (size of print, margins around print, one or two columns, headings). A grade of A, B, C, or D was given for this on the basis of how much the layout of the text made understanding easier.
Illustrations   (clarity, good labelling, the picture linking properly with the text)

Accuracy of information was also mentioned. This is more easily established in books about space or technology, as the date of publication gives a clue. Knowledge does not stand still in any area of learning, though. Current archaeological finds and interpretations can raise doubts about some of the information in older books. One way of looking at accuracy is to compare texts in different books.

The class textbook was also used for practice in making notes, though I did not find it very satisfactory for this. I would more often copy up passages from library books or make up my own passages on the subject. Textbooks do not often contain the balance between main ideas and details that other reference books have. Most books make a statement, reformulate it in a different way and 'pad out' round it to make the information clear and digestible. In most textbooks each short paragraph is made up of sentence/statements which are really a paragraph in themselves. The information is thus very dense and makes for difficult reading.

I had worked out a plan to help pupils with notemaking and note-taking which I had started to work through with the class: these short sessions were continued through the period of the project work.

Practice in making notes
Briefly these were the stages we followed:

1) I read aloud, the children followed the text, and then closed the books. I asked 'What do you remember?' and the pupils replied with anything they could think of. Finally I re-read the text.

2) The same procedure (as in 1), but with a discussion of the most important parts. I introduced the concepts 'main ideas' and 'details', explaining that the main ideas are the facts you need to understand about a subject (headings help a good deal to locate these) and the details are there to make the subject more interesting, but do not have to be learnt. I found with younger children this is a gradual process of understanding. The texts used initially must make the difference fairly obvious and the teacher may have to give heavy guidance at first. Often children *remember* little details better, and so get confused about their true importance.

3) We did the same again but this time children wrote down what they thought were the important parts. I helped the children to

use as few words as possible, just enough to remind them what they meant. They must use quick, not 'best', writing for this.

4) We repeated 3) — but with a time limit. I stressed that notes are for the pupil *only*, not for the teacher to assess. I gave pupils note books which they also used for jottings and reminders. These were their own property and I did not look into them without their consent.

5) I read through a passage aloud, then children used the text while they wrote the notes. The next day, children referred to notes and tried to talk about the main ideas. Then the original text was referred to for checking and discussion.

At any point two children can work together. For most pupils this is beneficial, as it can help less competent readers and provides an opportunity for informal preliminary discussion about main points and details.

7)   Presentation of work

We concluded the project with a presentation of the results displayed in the classroom. Each group was responsible for placing and arranging its own presentation. Nearly every group had attempted something different, drawn from our original list. One group came up with a new idea — a taped drama of food gathering and mealtimes! Children from other classes came and viewed the results in small groups at various times. The children learnt a great deal about presentation: making the writing large enough on a wall poster; making the important parts stand out; hanging posters straight and at eye level; presenting just the right amount of information on each poster; and many other points besides. Our last activity was to select some suitable items for storage for the next year's group to use.

8a)   Evaluation by the children

This was a very important part of the project. We discussed how each group's results might be evaluated and as a result drew up a document which was duplicated. This included headings such as accuracy of information, clarity, appeal, spelling, handwriting, appropriateness of mode of presentation and a space for passing on helpful hints. There was space beside each heading for comments and a grade.

Each group began by using the chart to evaluate their own work and then proceeded to other group's results. We did this in one hectic session which was not too serious. Each group ended up with evaluation sheets to look over and discuss.

I wanted to know how each pupil regarded the project and as well as discussing this everyone wrote briefly about their feelings towards this way of working. At this point I introduced a simple chart listing the ways in which, I felt, they could learn and asked each child to grade these ways from 1—10. These ways included reading, reading and note-making, discussing, asking a friend, asking at home, watching television, listening to the teacher talk, and copying from the board, (see Figure 2).

Ways of learning	
How do you learn: Which way do you think is best?	
Mark these ways of learning out of 10	
	Totals
1 Reading a book . . .	144
2 Listening to a tape . . .	158
3 Watching a television programme . . .	175
4 Talking and listening with friends . . .	90
5 Talking and listening with a group and the teacher . . .	176
6 Reading and copying from the blackboard . . .	136
7 Dictation . . .	55
8 Listening to the teacher explain things . . .	153
9 Doing workcards and worksheets with friends . . .	150
10 Doing workcards and worksheets alone . . .	109
11 Filling in missing words, talking about it . . .	142
12 Asking someone at home . . .	167

Figure 2

8b) Evaluation by the teacher

For my own evaluation I was concentrating on trying to assess how children were developing in the activities I had decided to focus on. These were:

a) skimming, scanning, and reading closely — being able to vary approach according to need,
b) using an index and contents page
c) making notes
d) being able to formulate specific questions
e) being able to plan an eventual presentation.

This was an informal assessment through observation while children were at work on the project. This seems to me to be the only sensible way to assess pupils' progress. Current tests that attempt to assess children's ability in reading for information are of two kinds. There is the series of tests within the APU (Assessment of Performance Unit) Language Test (2). These are *criterion referenced*. This means that the tests set out to see if a pupil can complete a task or not. The other kind of test is a *norm referenced* test, for example, the Language section of the Richmond Test (3). This kind of test sets out to separate children by their performance, and to put them in an order of merit according to predetermined norms for their age. Of course all tests, by their nature, are conducted in a very artificial situation with an imposed text. It would seem unlikely that such a test would give a realistic picture, tending to reflect the child's 'knowledge' rather than ability to use knowledge.

When I was observing children at work I would focus on, say, one group of two or three children. As well as observing I would build into our usual discussion some questions about their information-finding activities to establish if they had knowledge of techniques that I might not have seen them use.

At this time I was using a simple checklist for each pupil, as this was a fairly quick way of covering certain activities (Figure 3). I did find this device useful at the time, but because of its prescriptiveness I now prefer keeping a running commentary of observations and use it to build up a profile of each child over a period of time. The checklist I still find useful as a reminder of the aspects of reading for information that I want to concentrate on.

Organization and timetabling

The key word here is flexibility. I think that one of the most important factors that affects children's learning in the primary school is the timetable flexibility. This allows children to follow a natural learning pattern. Most people when faced with a long or short-term learning task would not choose a pattern of one session a week, as it has too many limitations. It is very important, therefore, that younger children can follow a varied pattern of time. This may contain longer and shorter sessions and should definitely include a strong element of choice and individual judgement. Fortunately, in the primary school we do not have to recognize rigid subject boundaries whereby children find it difficult to inter-relate ideas.

Sometimes we all worked on the project together, at other times only one or two groups were following the project while other groups or individuals were engaged in other activities. This, of course, eased the problem of resources. This class were accustomed to having a proportion of the day when they could plan and work independently within a prescribed schedule.

I have worked with children who were normally used to a high degree of teacher direction and a lot of drills and exercises in English. Such children initially need a lot of help and encouragement to work with someone else. With this group the children worked in pairs with a few children working on their own. The children are often

Reading: A Checklist			
Name . . . . Class . . . . Term . . . . . Eng 1/L, 2/L			

Reading for pleasure

Reads with interest and enjoyment
Reads at home
Goes to library
Reads a wide range of books
Favourite book
Can predict
Can recount story

Reading for information	Skill introduced	Competent	Skill used readily in other contexts
Goals			
Can set realistic goals			
Can break down goal into specific questions			
Planning			
Identifies likely resources			
Defines a suitable format for results			
Carrying out tasks			
Chooses 'suitable' books			
Makes good use of . . .			
Library classification			
Title			
Cover notes			
Index and contents			
Headings and other signposts			
Illustrations			
Skims, scans, reads closely			
Varies techniques above to fit task			
Produces a suitable result			
Development			
Can evaluate own work			
Can plan further developments			
Can use non-book resources			
(State which overleaf)			

Figure 3   A Checklist

uneasy about discussing and sharing ideas. They may be unused to talking in an exploratory, hesitant way, as their responses have been categorized as either right or wrong.

We all worked together on the project and for the first few sessions I would call a halt every half-hour or so to enquire how things were going. As the children got a firmer hold on this way of working they were anxious to break away from a set pattern and when this was not possible in school time, they would often work with each other at home.

Just as flexibility in timing and grouping is important, so is flexibility in the arrangement of the classroom and the use of space. For the duration of the project, display tables and various kinds of working areas are needed. These need not be in the classroom at all, in fact it is better if a space outside the classroom can be used.

Easy access to the school library is most helpful. It is difficult to encourage children to become independent and give them opportunities for acquiring and developing information skills if the library is often unavailable. Many schools timetable the library for class use for part of the week. Providing it is not too cramped, colleagues seldom object to one or two children looking for books or consulting reference books.

When the whole class are together, whether for discussion or brief reports, it is much more effective if the teacher has eye-contact with the whole group, and they all have eye-contact with each other. This usually involves moving the furniture around and it is tempting not to bother. It is easier if there is a break time either before or after such a session, then a group of children can make the necessary arrangements. I was interested in the research that found children to be getting on with their work more effectively when seated in rows rather than in groups (4). It must also be recognized that when children are seated in a circle with eye-contact they are better placed for learning through talk.

Children with learning/reading difficulties

Such children have not really been specifically mentioned so far. In the project I have described, they received a lot of help and support from other group members. In a good, co-operative working atmosphere more able children will and do give immeasurable help. This help is sometimes given consciously but often it is 'caught' by small group discussion and by more able children giving a model of good ways of working. If children with learning difficulties are grouped together (except at times when working with the teacher) they have little chance of learning from each other. They are deprived of this most potent means of learning.

In other projects or when working on topics that have more teacher input and direction, this group of children would have special material to work from. When working on a science topic, for instance, after the introduction and practical part of a session they have followed a task using a tape recorder and worksheet. The language-master, too, can be very useful here.

Children who are becoming bilingual

By the time they reach junior school, these children will be at very different stages in their use of English in the many different situations and curriculum areas, so we must look at individual needs. A Schools Council project relating to infant children has found that it is very important for children to work with peers who can show a good model of English spoken and written as a mother tongue (5).

In the early stages of our project the use of verbal and written questions was encouraged especially in groups containing pupils at an early stage of English acquisition. I also used some cloze texts with the whole class and would delete the verb in the past tense. In other topics some children would have special tape/worksheet material — this would include verbal repetition of phrases and sentences pointing out the areas of English language they had not fully grasped. The language would often be that which would be needed for specific curriculum areas such as science or history.

Conclusion

A summary of learning activities

I think it is useful at the end of a project to summarize the learning activities that it is hoped the children have engaged in. Here I would like to list the stages of planning, implementation and evaluation which are inherent in project work.

Reflecting on existing knowledge
Agreeing on broad goals
Breaking down broad goals into subgoals (their own particular area of enquiry)
Planning an outcome
Formulating specific questions
Speculating on possible sources of information
Planning division of enquiry
Working and discussing with friends
Summarizing progress and problems
Presenting an outcome
Evaluating their work and reflecting on their experience
Starting the next area of enquiry with the advantage of knowledge gained and the development of their information skills.

Some problems encountered

This project was by no means one hundred per cent 'successful'. There were times when I dearly wanted to revert to talk and chalk! Sometimes I was impatient with the 'diffuse' way in which children learn for themselves. It is much easier if the teacher tidily measures out portions of knowledge and children receive them in a set order. It all feels more secure and measurable — but children don't learn most effectively in that way!

I was sometimes concerned about the small amount of writing that went on. I remember once being particularly worried about a boy who experienced learning difficulties. He spent hours on his contribution towards a large plasticine model, with labels, of a settlement showing the animals and the people doing typical tasks. He had entered into much discussion around the subject while working and had shown much interest and understanding, but he had not produced any writing. I think, now, that junior school children are often required to do too much writing, sometimes without very good reasons. Looking back on that boy, it seemed that talk, while working and reworking that scene, generated his understanding and conversely, the completed scene demonstrated his understanding, as writing could not have done.

Again I remember vividly the number of times individual children approached me, with enquiries about their part of the group's work. 'Have you talked to the others in your group?', 'No', 'Well go and talk to them and try to sort it out between you.' I felt very exasperated about this at times but on reflection, younger children do like to have the individual attention of their teacher and they do sometimes find it difficult to consult and perhaps to value the judgement of their peers.

Three factors: content, process and product

The finished products of this project were not perfect by any means, and of course many were not of the type to be taken home to gather dust in a forgotten corner of a bedroom! The act of balancing the 'process' with the 'product' is difficult. Also there is the question of 'Is there a body of knowledge which must be learnt?' I don't think that these three factors are mutually exclusive.

Project work should not exclude contributions from the teacher, perhaps through the introduction or a rounding up and a putting into perspective at the end. I also think that the teacher must be aware of and gradually make children aware of the special disciplines of subjects. In history, for example, the differences between primary and secondary sources and cause and effect, and in science, hypothesis and deductive reasoning must be covered.

The process, I believe, is all important, especially with younger children. The processes by which children learn cannot be developed in a vacuum so the focus of their learning must be interesting and absorbing. Children and adults naturally want to see some kind of end product for their efforts. Parents, too, naturally like to see evidence of learning. It is surely a question of balancing process and product and a question of negotiating goals with children. It is good for children and parents to know that the teacher has clear underlying aims for reading and general language development, and has planned activities to implement these aims. The teacher, on his or her part, can recognize the sense of achievement that children feel when they produce something that is the result of collaboration and effort. Teachers and pupils should be partners in learning.

5

Problem solving

So far we have discussed information skills in terms of finding out from books. Alphabet practice and dictionary games have as an implicit end the mastery of written work. The topic work in the previous chapter did include the development of oral skills and group work, but much of what was accomplished involved learning from printed sources and producing written work. This is entirely understandable since the idea of independent learning is still largely based on the use of the printed and written word.

However, books are not necessarily or even usually the first resort of a majority of people when seeking information (see Chapter 4, Figure 1). Asking someone or listening to an expert is still the most popular way of discovering information. However, the essence of successful information skills practice is to tackle any information problem by analysing the steps needed to find a solution. The 'Nine steps' are quoted in the Schools Council Curriculum Bulletin, 9, and may be summarized here as

what do I want to know
how can I find out
what should I do with this information

This is a problem-solving formula which applies equally well to information received from books, people or any other sources. The solution to the problem will lie in assessing all the information received, and reaching a decision based on interpreting that information in a way that answers the specific need.

The next chapter describes such a problem-solving exercise in a primary school. The issue to be resolved was the reorganization of playground space, and the children were able to present a solution that was both practical and popular with their schoolmates.

In order to solve the problem it was necessary to define it, to collect evidence and opinions from other members of the school and analyse it, to think about it from several different angles and discuss them in groups. In the process, skills of information gathering, collation and evaluation were being practised, as well as mathematical ones in measuring and calculating.

Finally, the solution had to be 'sold' to the school using the skill of presenting information as evidence.

Making such an exercise possible requires much support and planning by the teacher. The traditional role of imparter of knowledge is abandoned temporarily for that of guide, adviser and even onlooker. However, the teacher also needs to be the assessor of the exercise, as Pauline demonstrates.

One other important factor to which she draws attention is the need for the support of the rest of the school, particularly the head, to make such an exercise practicable.

5

Problem solving

Pauline Millward

Introduction

I teach in a purpose-built open-plan junior school which was opened in 1972. It is situated on the outskirts of a large industrial conurbation, has a two-form entry and serves a very large and mixed catchment area. We try to match our curriculum to the diversity of needs, stressing learning rather than 'leading'. Although there are many demands imposed by the conflicting needs of flexibility for independent learning and structure for monitoring individual progress, we try to blend and balance these through our study skills programme.

The staff are encouraged to apply our extensive study skills programme to all curriculum areas. This involves reading skills, such as being able to pick out the main idea(s) of a passage, paragraph, chapter or book; being able to list important relevant details which support and underline the main idea; being able to pick out one or more key words in a question, to enable them to choose the right book, and look up the right word in the book's index, or contents page. They should also be able to look for key phrases in a passage which will guide them to an answer. It includes the various stages of skimming, scanning, questioning, reviewing, cross referencing, discerning fact from opinion, developing location skills for finding information, reading graphs, maps, charts, and of course all forms of writing. In topic work especially, the work is directed towards the use of these research techniques. The success is measured by how well they are used, developed and extended rather than by the number of facts remembered. The development of these skills is very important to the children if they are to achieve future success in this type of learning, and develop the capacity for absorbing a greater depth and width of knowledge (1, 2, 3).

What is 'real' problem solving?

'Real' problem solving is best described as an approach to learning through direct experience of a problem which is 'real' to the learner; the means of arriving at a solution through trial and error, which will be beneficial to them in their daily life, and develop their thinking, mathematically, logically and linguistically (4). As a format for practising thinking and developing organizational skills, it is convenient in that there is a defined objective. Whether the objective is achieved is not so important as the methods used in attempting to achieve it. It should not, however, be thought of as the sole means of developing thinking, or considered in isolation from other thinking processes and skills. It is merely another way of demonstrating these processes (5).

Where do I begin with problem solving?

I have been including problem solving in my curriculum programme for the past five years, following involvement with the Open University Mathematics Team who were developing an INSET Course P.M.E. 233 *Mathematics Across the Curriculum* and organizing an intensive training session through my LEA. I discovered many possibilities and opportunities for learning offered by this approach. Children were not only encouraged to use relevant acquired skills and concepts, but also to develop reasoning ability and lively, inquiring minds, with an appetite for further knowledge, not limited by subject boundaries. The vastness of this potential became more obvious as I became increasingly involved.

The 'real' problem to be outlined here was undertaken by the children because it was *important to them* and they had a real interest in resolving the situation. They *valued* the outcome. In short, *they felt involved.*

A problem solving project in school

The children in school were dissatisfied with playtime as it was for a number of sensible reasons, but when some of them showed a great dislike for playtime it appeared to be a real problem area which needed investigation. It was decided to discover why this was so, and to recommend possible ways of improvement, so that everyone could have the opportunity of enjoying their free time.

The problem

The playing area is divided into two parts. There is one large tarmacked area at the rear of the school. To reach this, half of the children have to walk all the way round the school building and go down some steps. The playing area itself, owing to a land fault, is exactly level with the top of the fences in the surrounding gardens, with a steep slope at one end. This means that footballs are constantly being lost. In this playground are two pieces of climbing apparatus, one large and one small, and there is a variety of grid markings on the surface.

The other play area is much smaller and is situated at the side of the school. It is surrounded by grassed areas. There is no apparatus here and only a few grid markings. To reach this spot all of the children have to walk around part of the school building.

The children in my class who were to tackle the problem were aged nine and ten years and of mixed ability. They had had no previous experience in group work of this nature, or of enquiry procedure, and were to find it a very rewarding and purposeful part of the project. No-one envisaged the tremendous skill-using and skill-getting which was to be involved.

The problems acronym

Once the problem has been selected various stages of progression need to be organized in order to arrive at a solution. The method I have found to be most useful is the one recommended by the Open University (6) and involves the following acronym:

P Posing the problem
R Refining your ideas
O Outlining the questions to ask
B Bringing the right data home
L Looking for solutions
E Establishing the recommendations
M Making it happen
S So what next?

Posing the problem or introducing the challenge

Having identified the playground area as a problem within the school, the children now had to convince the other members of the school community of its relevance to them by providing evidence and attempting to arrive at a solution. The wording chosen for the challenge was: *'How to make playtime more interesting for everyone'*.

A great deal of discussion followed during a 'brain-storming' session. Each child put forward any ideas he or she had as to why playtime was so unsatisfactory to him or her. These ideas were just listed haphazardly in order of suggestion, not in any logical or pre-planned groupings. Every point was included, however relevant or irrelevant it may have appeared.

The children were now ready to plan their investigations into the problem.

Refining the areas for investigation or planning the programme

Again the whole class was involved in this stage of the project, where they regrouped their haphazard list into logical units for investigation. This was done systematically through the use of a topic web. By writing the challenge in the centre and by careful questioning, such as 'Which of the suggestions on this list do you think we could group together? Are there any others we could put together under a different heading?', the children were able to identify four main areas for their new lists. These were:

1) What is wrong with playtime?
2) Organization of the large playing area.
3) Games and activities.
4) Planning the small playing area.

Now the children needed to be organized into groups to enable them to plan their investigations. The four areas of investigation were carried out simultaneously and the findings from each one integrated with the other areas.

Outlining the questions to ask

Here the children within each group discussed possible questions they considered would be relevant to obtain information needed to help them with their task. They had to anticipate whether the answers would help to solve their part of the problem, or if in fact they would be able to find any answers at all.

They then came back together as a whole class once more for further discussion.

Bringing the right data home

The ideas from each group were pooled and discussed by the class, until a rationalized approach was agreed upon for each area of investigation. This was to ensure that the information collection was not duplicated and that job allocation was organized to produce maximum effort and maximum results. Organized methods for sharing information and for interaction between the groups were also planned. These were to be short reporting-back sessions at each stage of the project, allowing children from all groups to express their views upon the area being discussed. Different groups also needed to co-operate at various intervals throughout the project in order to get the most satisfactory results for their part of the challenge.

It was decided that the first group, 'What is wrong with playtime?' and the third group, 'Games and activities', needed to design a question-naire for the whole school in order to find out what the other children thought about playtime. They also needed to survey the existing activities at playtime and to interview the teaching and non-teaching staff.

This approach would enable them:

1) to gain evidence, in a systematic manner, of any likes and dislikes of playtime activities experienced by the other children;

2) to consider opinions other than their own;

3) to work together in small groups.

The possible problems which could arise were discussed by the whole class before the first group actually began to design and prepare the questionnaire for both areas of the problem (7). This was begun with guidance from the head teacher.

Taking into account the children's capabilities, the time available to carry out the survey, the time each child could be given to fill in their answers, and the depth of answers required, it was important that they were given guidance at this stage. Particular attention was given to the following points:

1) What do you most dislike about playtime?

2) What do you like about playtime?

3) What would you like to see happening at playtime?

When the questionnaire had been prepared, the questions were far from perfect, but this was expected. A 'trial run' was given to their own group, which helped to clarify some of the difficulties and the questions were re-phrased accordingly.

The completed questionnaire was now duplicated and administered throughout the school by children themselves.

The analysis of the results proved a very difficult task, as each child had written out a list of likes and dislikes, and therefore there was a great deal of repetition. The group made a list of the 'dislikes' (fighting, boredom, ball games, etc.), made a tally of them, and then recorded their findings on a graph. Care was needed to ensure concise presentation of results in order to draw critical comparisons.

They repeated this for 'likes' and for 'games and activities' and passed on the information to the appropriate group. Analysis and presentation of the results were now quickly achieved and made ready for use. The development of this difficult skill has been explained in full because it proved to be the most challenging task of all during the problem.

The other groups were all involved in the learning of new skills. They needed to know how to make a plan of the school using scale drawing; how to measure large areas; how to observe the activities of other children; how to interview children and adults; how to cost materials and estimate the quantities needed. Another difficult area was designing the use of the space available as it involved being able to envisage what the final play areas would look like. Other skills such as computation, volume, money and percentages were used too, but the children had some previous experience in these areas. It was important to stress to the children the need for consistency and accuracy in all aspects of their work.

When all of the necessary information had been collected the groups were ready for the next stage in their problem solving.

Looking for solutions

The information which each group now had was analysed and interpreted by that group so possible recommendations could be made. These were:

1) If all ball games were restricted to the large playground, then children who did not like ball games could play in the small playground without interference.
2) If the small apparatus was removed from the large play area, then more children would use it, leaving more space for ball games.
3) If the hop-scotch grids were painted in the small play area instead of the large one, then they could be used without spoiling the ball games or the fear of being pushed over.
4) If a fence was erected between the infant school canteen and the house gardens at the bottom of the playground, then the infant children would not spoil the games in the large play area.
5) If a hill was put near the small play area on the grass, then the children who wished to play with toy cars would not interfere with other games.
6) If a ten-foot fence was put around the large playground, then this would prevent footballs going into gardens.
7) If all of these recommendations were operational then playtime would be a happier time for everyone.

Establishing the recommendations

These recommendations were discussed by the whole class and jobs allocated for putting them into effect. A written report, detailing these recommendations with justifications, was produced and then Mr Smith was approached to request a 'trial run'. There was only one slight alteration in the final list, and that was in recommendation 5. He suggested that perhaps the hole left by the soil to be used for the hill could be filled with sand and used as a sand-pit. Permission was granted for the implementation of the recommendations, so the children were ready to begin putting them into effect.

Making it happen

The children in the class, with help from Mr Smith, moved the small apparatus as planned.

A group designed and painted hop-scotch grids on the small play area and surrounding paths. They also painted a road for toy cars. Each child had a turn at digging the sand-pit and making the hill.

An additional problem here was working out the volume of sand required and the costing of it. The children worked this out by themselves and submitted the figures to Mr Smith who saw to the purchasing.

The fence required for separating the infants from the juniors was measured and costed. It was eventually donated by a parent.

The ten-foot fence, unknown to the children, had already been recommended and agreed upon by the Local Education Authority.

Now the children were ready for action. The whole school was assembled and selected representatives explained the results of the survey and the recommendations. The new system of playtime was to be tried out for one week and was to be put into effect immediately.

The actual outcome surprised everyone, including the children. Each recommendation worked well and the children appeared to be enjoying themselves. After a week the situation was reviewed and it was decided to keep the system in operation as it had proved so successful. The children had managed to find a suitable solution to their problem and experienced the satisfaction of seeing it operate — pupils were now enjoying playtime.

The actual work produced by the children was displayed for people to read, as each aspect had involved all of the school at some level, and obviously had created a great deal of interest. This boosted the confidence of the children and gave them a real sense of achievement. They gained sufficient confidence to talk to adults about their work and were happy to address the whole school and staff in an assembly. The whole project had taken five weeks from start to finish, with the children working approximately four hours per week.

In a school with such a diverse community, this first attempt at problem solving served as a useful educational development. This was achieved by involving all of the children and providing them with the opportunity of experiencing aspects of school life in which they had previously never needed to become involved.

The playtime project was a success because the children enjoyed it and felt they had solved their problem. They had applied basic educational skills to a real situation which had motivated them towards learning.

Evaluation of a problem-solving project

Evaluation is a very important part of any innovation, in this instance problem solving, for by learning through first-hand experience what will or will not work helps to develop a much stronger foundation for future situations.

I needed to evaluate this work for three reasons:

1) it represented a significant part of the term's work;
2) to find out if any aspects required re-thinking or improvement;
3) to assess what each child had gained from the experience. (**8, 9, 10.**)

The format needed to be continuous, concise and comprehensive. As real problem solving is open-ended, there are plenty of chances for children to use their skills or acquire new ones, even if these are not planned directly. Careful observation of individual reactions to particular situations enables an assessment to be made of each individual's stage of development.

Individual diagnostic observations helped to foster the development of each child by providing an overall picture of his or her strengths and weaknesses. This overall view was taken into account when planning individual programmes of work. A great deal was learned from the behaviour of each child during group activities. This helped during future organization of small groups by obviating certain problems and encouraging social development.

Cumulative records of work and performance were kept for every child, to indicate how well concepts, mathematical skills, logical thinking, and language skills had been mastered. The records included both areas which were already well-developed and were being used with confidence, and skills which had been needed, but could not be used independently and required further work or individual help. They also indicated areas where skill acquisition would be advantageous.

A note was made of any noticeable gains in skills, abilities and confidence that the child acquired during the project. Any skills or abilities required for the project which had not been taught were noted for future classwork, and assessment of the adequacy of the child's problem-solving skills was recorded. Any part of the process of the 'problems' acronym which required special attention with the whole class was also observed and noted.

These results helped considerably when arranging further curriculum work so that maximum benefits would be obtained. The most useful tool in planning future work was the grid for skill acquisition (Figure 1) as it helped to clarify the situation and forecast possible conceptual developments to be encountered during the problem-solving project. This grid can be adapted for use in any of the curriculum areas, but it must be emphasized that it is only a preliminary guide, and many skills and concepts will be used which have not been included.

The teacher's role

During the course of the project it became obvious that the role of the teacher was extremely important. As well as having to be well-organized, the teacher needed to act as a *creator*, a *facilitator* and an *intervener*.

1)   The creator of the learning climate

Creating a learning environment was of prime concern and was difficult in that it had to be child-centred the whole time in order to avoid the teacher becoming a central processor of the children's ideas. The development of the pupils' thinking process had to be predominant in all of the

Opportunities for skill acquisition

Skill/concept likely to be needed	Probable teaching unit	Probable point of introduction	Resource which may be helpful
Observation and recording information	Small group	At the beginning of project	Worksheets
How to design and conduct an opinion survey	Small group	As needed	Worksheets
Scale drawing, planning	Small group	As needed	SMP* cards
How to organize equipment, etc	Whole class	As needed	
How to conduct interviews with adults and children	Individuals	As needed	
How to produce a topic web	Whole class	At the beginning of the project	Worksheets

* SMP is the School Mathematics Project 7–13 and is the core of the school's mathematics curriculum. Any mathematics scheme would be appropriate.

Figure 1

learning situations which were organized. This aspect of teaching was the most taxing, but was ultimately the most rewarding, although even when the project was near completion it was still difficult to create a completely independent learning situation each time.

The children had to be made to feel confident that any ideas they had to offer would not lead to a loss of face. They needed encouragement to realize that there was no risk involved in making a contribution and that it would be positively valued.

Encouraging the children to have ideas of their own and displaying a willingness to accept what they had to offer were two aspects of the creator role. There were others, however, which could be considered as having made an even greater contribution to making the children feel that the responsibility to solve the problem was really theirs.

The children were allowed to make their own mistakes and find their own way. The teacher's responsibility was not to solve the problem, but to encourage the children to find their own solution. The emphasis was on collaboration rather than directing the children towards a solution.

Child—child interaction, instead of child—teacher interaction was another important aspect offered. The children had to be given the chance to exercize their own judgement and a conscious effort had to be made to ensure this. By avoiding the pitfall of becoming a 'central processor' the appropriate environment for real problem solving was created.

2)   The facilitator of the problem-solving process

This role encouraged the problem-solving process by co-ordinating, amongst other things, the flow between small group work and whole class discussion. Sufficient time had to be made available for the children to become involved in the problem. Two sessions each week with time between for the children to mull over the problem was found to be most successful.

Another aspect was checking with colleagues in advance to see if it would be all right for the children to go into other classes to collect information. The head teacher had to be kept informed at each stage to avoid placing him in an embarrassing situation. The use of resources not normally available to the children, like the use of the duplicator or the telephone, also had to be arranged.

As a 'facilitator' the co-ordination of the children's work was involved. This was to ensure that effort was not duplicated and groups whose investigations were interdependent were kept informed of one another's progress. Interaction between groups was a vital element in maintaining the momentum of the real problem project. Report-back meetings were organized at the end of each session so that the small groups could meet together to discuss progress, re-focus on the challenge, and not lose sight of the overall goal.

3)   The intervener in the learning process

Intervening required a questioning technique which would put the onus on the children to do the thinking rather than relying upon the teacher to supply the answers. As in all teaching, there were many points during the projects where teacher intervention was necessary for one reason or another. It was absolutely vital to try to get the children to do the thinking in order to develop their problem-solving ability. To do this, 'open-ended' questions were essential in order to enable the children to reason and formulate their own thoughts. The teacher was required to 'think on his feet' in front of the class and so guide the children towards the necessary thinking.

The children could not be told *what* to think. Early in the project they needed help in being shown *how* to think as they lacked experience in solving problems. Intervention was needed in the processes of their thought, not in the conclusions.

I found this a complex role, as I was often tempted to intervene when a group was unable to see an obvious point or solution. I had to remind myself that it was not my place to solve the problem, that was definitely the children's task.

Conclusion

Throughout the project the children received the support of the other children, the teachers, the head teacher, and each other. Without this co-operation the whole project would not have been viable, as the challenge and areas for investigation were dependent upon information gained from the questionnaires.

The mathematical and linguistic thinking processes which were employed throughout were recorded and communicated to the head teacher and colleagues. The skill-getting and skill-using method was discussed and evaluated also in tabulated form. The number of skills recorded exceeded any pre-conceived lists.

So what next?

Since this first attempt at problem solving, I have encouraged the other members of staff to try it with their classes. Although a bit reluctant at first, a few of them did accept the idea and were very pleasantly surprised by their results. Like me, they found the most difficult part to be that of intervener, as they were so used to giving advice and answering queries.

This was also the case with teachers I have encountered during in-service courses. The other main difficulty is actually finding a problem for the children to solve. If the children do not offer any suggestions immediately, then use local newspapers for articles which may affect their lives out of school, but above all which are important to them. For example, this could be the closure of a youth centre, or the need for a pelican crossing on a nearby road. Should this not supply an answer, then a problem could be the challenge of organizing a sports day, a tuck shop, a Christmas party, making the best use of classroom space, or how to arrange the cloakroom more efficiently. I have tackled several of these with various classes, and in most cases found a satisfactory answer to the problem. Those that did not work out were not due to the children's inability to find a solution, but because the project was not viable financially. In one case the children did suggest that they make fund-raising their next problem to solve, so that they could complete the first! It was at this point that I realised fully how resourceful children could be, and also how mature they become when faced with the fact that their project could not be made to work, despite their hard work.

Simulation

I have recently helped to organize a problem-solving course of a different nature to the previous ones. This involved the use of drama as a means of posing the problem. Whilst I believe that there is no substitute for 'real' problem solving, there is an additional skill to be used through the medium of drama, that of projection. By attempting to solve a problem through simulation the children can be made aware of cultural difficulties, morality, and socialization. For example, the children may be studying the North American Indians in their project work. The problem could be for them to become the tribe whose chief had died, and as members of the senior council, to decide how they are going to select a new one. This would involve research into the tribal laws and general lifestyle of the Indians before the class could even begin to find a solution. Other skills would probably include election procedures, tallying, discussions, logical reasoning, role play, and identification of qualities needed by the Chief. It would also involve some use of history and geography skills.

A checklist of important points

A useful way of summarizing this chapter, I feel, is to outline the suggested framework for guiding teacher's actions during problem solving, as proffered by practising teachers, and the Open University (6).

Planning a problem

There are several questions which you must ask yourself at the outset.

1) Are the tasks likely to achieve satisfactory results?
2) Will the task be of sufficient interest to the children?
3) Do I have, or can I obtain access to adequate resources?
4) What resources will I need to create to achieve the objective?
5) Are the children able to cope with the resources?
6) What skills might I need to teach the children so that they can make full use of the resources?
7) Do the children have the skills, knowledge and experience which are a necessary pre-requisite for attempting the task?
8) Will the task provide a good opportunity for teaching a skill or developing a concept?

It is important to remember that the *context* will provide the *purpose* which will *facilitate* skill-using and *motivate* skill-acquisition.

Some constraints which may apply might be:

The children themselves
1) How experienced are they in participating in discussion?

2) Have they any experience of co-operating with others to achieve a common goal?

3) What experience have they of observing?

4) How experienced are they in asking questions that may lead to the exploration and understanding of a new experience?

5) Have they any experience in directing the pace of their learning?

6) Have they experience in persevering towards achieving a goal?

The curriculum

What are the requirements of other curricular demands on the children, the teacher and the school timetable? The amount of time available for problem solving and the degree of flexibility for use of this time is very important.

The materials

The equipment that is available or accessible for measuring, recording, reprographics, and so on. (Look out for deficiences rather than those in use).

The school

You will need:

1) The support of the head teacher.

2) The support of other teachers.

3) To be aware of the attitude of people not on the staff.

4) To know the building itself and its difficulties.

5) To know the requirements of supervision of children within the school and outside school and to have the scope for obtaining the necessary help to satisfy these requirements.

The teacher

You must be aware of your expectations of what particular children might be able to achieve. Three levels of difficulty were thought to be important.

1) The *independent* stage, when the child is confident about using skills and coping without help.

2) The *instructional* stage, when the child is able to cope with the task *with* the teacher's help.

3) The *frustration* stage, when the task is beyond the child's present capabilities.

This awareness will help to diagnose difficulties and determine appropriate teaching strategies such as:

Frustration level — alter approach to the problem.
Instructional level — skill-getting approach.
Independent level — skill-using approach.

The three dimensions mentioned earlier in the chapter are important to remember when you are considering what you may need to do, as *the creator* of the the learning climate; as *the facilitator* of the problem solving process, and as *an intervener* in the learning process.

The teacher is *not* the problem solver.

6

Integrating the microcomputer into information skills teaching

One of the new areas of challenge in education is the introduction of the microcomputer into schools. Many teachers have reacted enthusiastically to this challenge, but others are dubious about its place in the curriculum, especially in the primary school. There is also the problem of acquiring competence in the use of microcomputers and a knowledge of appropriate software. Fortunately, there is help in this area from the MEP regional centres (1) and many LEAs where in-service courses are being developed for teachers, to include the evaluation and provision of software. In addition many teachers' centres and school library services have software for loan or inspection.

One potential use of microcomputers for information skills teaching is their ability to store and manipulate large amounts of information. Therefore, as the next chapter shows, the facts collected as part of topic work can be used to test a variety of hypotheses in a way not possible previously without hours of tedious work. Compiling one's own database provides a valuable insight into how information can be processed and manipulated and also shows the computer will only yield information that is as good as it receives.

Another powerful use is as a simulator to develop the ability of children to make decisions and predict consequences based on known facts — a machine version of problem solving in fact, but giving instant feedback if wrong decisions are made.

It is essential that the microcomputer is welcomed into the classroom as another learning tool. It can be used very successfully in topic work alongside more 'conventional' methods, as this chapter shows.

6

Integrating the microcomputer into information skills teaching

Martin Jackson

The school

My school is a Church of England (voluntary controlled) combined school with some two hundred and thirty children in the first school and a further two hundred and forty pupils in the middle school. It offers excellent facilities for today's primary school children, and particularly relevant here, a Mathematics Laboratory was created in 1982 and a twelve-bay Spectrum 48K, Computer Laboratory was installed in 1983.

Micro resources

An enthusiastic and hard-working Friends of the School association and a local charity have made it possible for the school to purchase a further ten micros for classroom use in addition to those in the computer laboratory. Eight of these are BBC Model B's and two are Spectrum 48K machines. Additional micro hardware consists of a printer, word-processing chips, disk-drives, an acoustic coupler, a Prestel teletext receiver, concept keyboards and a special Visi-speech unit for help with our partially-hearing pupils who suffer with speech related difficulties.

Software and the Energy project

Our software library contains hundreds of programs and represents a broad spectrum of the educational programs available to schools, which stretch across the entire breadth of the curriculum. When an 'Energy' project for third and fourth year middle school pupils was proposed I undertook that aspect of the project for which we had a seemingly tailor-made computer program. British Petroleum had produced a learning pack and program based on a board game where the players had to combat and control an oil-slick off the coast of Scotland. The program is called *Slick* (2).

As the broad aim of the project was for the children to learn about energy production and to discover for themselves the importance of conservation, I began to plan my contribution to include other computer programs in addition to *Slick*.

Choosing the programs

I consider that the classroom micro is invaluable for information skills teaching. These children were used to collecting and handling data, both on traditional lines with card-index files and by using *Factfile* (3), a program designed to introduce information handling on the micro. This MEP program is very good as an introduction to data-base teaching, but because I wanted to develop the children's already-acquired basic skills I decided to offer them a more complex program called *Inform* (4). This is much faster than *Factfile* and has much greater capacity and flexibility.

A specific aim of my part of the project was to underline the importance of energy control and conservation using the skills of information gathering and sorting, with the micro assisting to develop the children's skills of data-interpretation and deduction even further. It occurred to me that we ought to use the micro as part of our presentation at the conclusion of the project. After all, viewdata is rapidly becoming commonplace in our society and the project seemed an ideal way of introducing completely new skills.

Flow charting

After formulating ideas about how we were going to approach the project, I drew up a final flow chart. I find that using flow charts in the planning stage of any project is a most useful way of presenting ideas. Then, as a second stage of planning, I examined every aspect of the project shown on the flow diagram to explore how each one might be developed. The key gives an indication of how this was achieved and sketches out some of the ways in which the project could progress, incorporating the use of acquired skills such as creative writing, research skills in using the library, and the acquisition of new skills, represented by the various computer programs selected.

Class organization

It was important for a two-term project with the fourth year pupils to consider how best the project could be undertaken. Should the class follow a set pattern of objectives with every child covering the same ground? Or, considering the vast scope the project offered, should I split the class into groups with each one working on different aspects of the whole, using different resources, and then bring the project together at the end with a series of group presentations? I decided on the latter, as I have found that projects of this kind give the opportunity for every child to produce something worthwhile, which is not in any way diminished in value by the inevitable comparisons that are evident when the former approach is used. Accordingly, the class was divided into groups of mixed

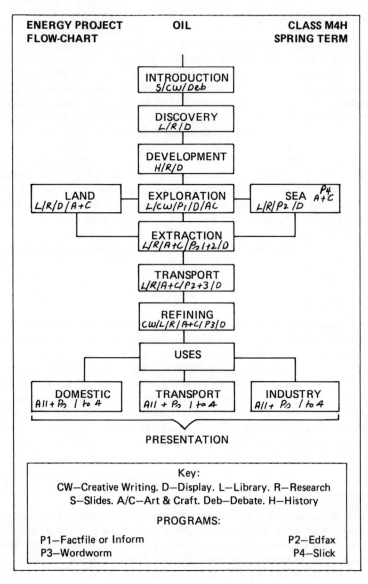

ENERGY PROJECT
FLOW-CHART

OIL

CLASS M4H
SPRING TERM

INTRODUCTION
S/CW/Deb

DISCOVERY
L/R/D

DEVELOPMENT
H/R/D

LAND
L/R/D/A+C

EXPLORATION
L/CW/P₁/D/AC

SEA *P4*
L/R/P₂/D *A+C*

EXTRACTION
L/R/A+C/P₂1+2/D

TRANSPORT
L/R/A+C/P2+3/D

REFINING
CW/L/R/A+C/P3/D

USES

DOMESTIC
All + P₂ 1 to 4

TRANSPORT
All + P₂ 1 to 4

INDUSTRY
All+ P₂ 1 to 4

PRESENTATION

Key:
CW—Creative Writing. D—Display. L—Library. R—Research
S—Slides. A/C—Art & Craft. Deb—Debate. H—History

PROGRAMS:

P1—Factfile or Inform   P2—Edfax
P3—Wordworm   P4—Slick

Figure 1

ability. Six groups of five children seemed an ideal way of dividing up the work once the introductory stages of the project were completed.

The project as a whole was outlined and discussed in the following lesson and the class divisions were made. I was careful to ensure as far as possible that each group was made up of children who could make positive contributions to their own group. In addition I was determined to watch carefully to ensure that the less able were not overshadowed by their brighter colleagues and reduced to performing the more mundane tasks for the group's eventual presentation. The six groups were told that they had to vary their presentations and could choose from a variety of formats which ranged from booklets through sound tapes, to illustrated talks or Ceefax pages. Alternatively, a mixture of presentations could be used.

Resource materials

Over the years, the school, like most others, has built up its own collection of resource materials. Any new project leads to the acquisition of resources of all kinds — some purchased and others given free-of-charge. Teachers are natural collectors and items once acquired may be saved for use time and time again.

Our school has a large room, which houses catalogued materials suited for all kinds of projects, from packs on Roman Britain to space exploration. The careful preservation of such materials proves invaluable in giving the class teachers an opportunity to mount initial displays suited to a current project.

Such a display had already been mounted using resources on Energy available in the school and it was suggested that each group could add to the display as part of their presentation, or in a more general sense by bringing along anything pertinent they might have access to at home or from the results of their researches. Every child had a simplified copy of the flow chart, and material present on the display tables disappeared as each group began to plan their contributions. This was quite a noisy session but as I moved from group to group I realized that the children were excited at the prospect of a new project, and that the noise was only the consequence of every one of them wanting to make a contribution.

Areas of investigation

Each group came up with diverse ideas, such as building databases on quantities of oil produced by different companies in the North Sea; the garages in our town, and the different kinds of fuel used in domestic heating. These two were designed to find out which garage offered the biggest range of petrols and oils at the best prices and to see if oil as a home heating source was more popular than other energy fuels. The first databases required letters requesting information on North Sea oil production from the major petro-chemical companies. These produced a huge amount of booklets, posters and, in one case, a sample of oil from the companies, most of which was free!

The two groups investigating garages used *Factfile* to compile their

databases. The first group discovered that they required a database program which would give them more scope to handle the vast amount of
information they had received. This was an opportunity to introduce
Inform and required a couple of lunch-hours teaching them how to use a
disk drive so that they could proceed. It took this particular group some
time to sort out exactly how they were going to process their information
in a format which was easy to enter and subsequently easily interrogated
and in order to save time I had to give them quite a lot of direction at
this initial stage.

Using the micro

Edfax

All the groups wanted to use *Edfax* as their sole means of presentation.
This was following a lesson where we had examined the program's facilities. *Edfax* is a program which simulates the Ceefax and Oracle viewdata
services of the BBC and ITV television companies respectively. With
Edfax, children can create their own 'pages' (one full TV screen) of
information, complete with their own illustrative graphics. Since Ceefax
presentation was new and exciting, everyone wanted to use it for their
group. This presented quite a problem, which I overcame by laying down
the groundrule that information had to be well-researched, and first
presented in a more traditional way. After being passed by the referee —
myself — the group was allowed to try using Ceefax. The children soon
realized that it wasn't quite as easy as they had imagined, and that preparing Ceefax pages was time-consuming. An allowance per group of between
two and five pages had to be stipulated, as I wished to use the two micros
available for the other programs.

Wordworm

One group came up with an idea for using a program in connection with
the project which I hadn't considered at all. In another class the children
had used a spelling program called *Wordworm* (6) in which children
could enter and save their own spelling lists. It was suggested that a spelling
data list of all the new and sometimes lengthy words which the children
were coming across, many for the first time, could be created for general
use. I agreed that this would be a good idea, as the program was a game
where letters of a particular word were spread across the screen at random
and the operator had to use a growing worm to eat the letters of the word
in the right order of spelling. I thought that the value of the exercise was
not so much in the playing of the game as what went into the preparation
and the data bank. The group duplicated data-sheets for themselves and
the other groups to use as the project progressed. Children entered new

words on their sheets as they came across them and also their meanings. At the end of each lesson the sheets were handed in, and at the beginning of the following week's lesson a few minutes were taken up by the group concerned in selecting words for the *Wordworm* database. As new words were fed into the program and saved on a weekly basis I was pleased to see that all five members of this group were taking a turn at this task on the micro. Only a few members of the class were capable of writing programs in Basic but even the least able were able to change data statements in the *Wordworm* program and grew considerably more confident as they did so. It was quite obvious that these children gained a great deal of satisfaction and pleasure from this exercise — one boy even said 'It makes me feel important'. The game itself was played at break times only, each group in turn, and I was pleased to see that over the course of the term the children' spellings of the specialist vocabulary in the databank improved greatly, although, as one would naturally suppose, the more usual spelling errors were still in evidence!

Using *Slick*

The groups were progressing well except for one which had elected to try a radio documentary type presentation. This group was discovering that selection of information and scripting was not as easy as they had thought. The father of one of the boys worked for a company which manufactured and installed computerised oil pumping stations in the Arabian Gulf countries and had invited the group to visit the company. The children interviewed him on tape but in the event this was a limited success as he was too technical in his explanations. The group was becoming very dispirited and losing interest, particularly as they watched the enjoyment of their colleagues involved in presentations with more freedom and variety of approach.

I was wondering when I could introduce the fourth computer program *Slick*, so it seemed appropriate to do so now with this particular group. *Slick*, produced by British Petroleum, is a simulation of an oil tanker disaster in the North Sea, off the east coast of Scotland. The idea of the program is that, with information given and resources selected, the user has to combat an oil slick of one hundred tonnes, located some sixty miles east of a beautiful Scottish fishing town. The slick is threatening fishing grounds, tourist beaches, bird sanctuaries and nature conservation areas.

This first group of six children to be introduced to the program were very excited and quickly absorbed the information given to them to operate the program. Colourful maps of the area, called Northsands Bay, were supplemented with duplicated maps for mapping the course of the oil slick. Data sheets giving information about the various methods of dealing with oil pollution at sea and on land were read and discussed. The children realized immediately that to use a sinking method over fishing grounds

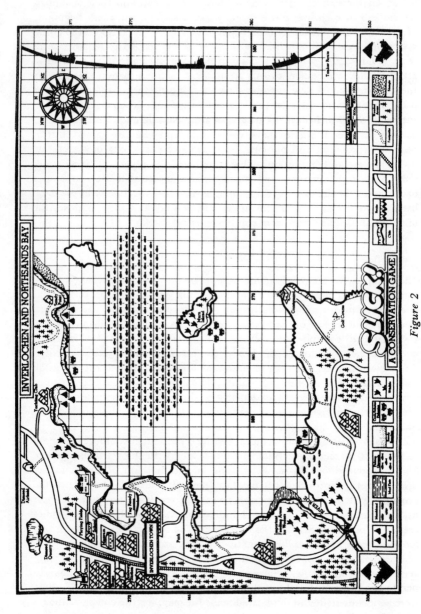

Figure 2

Reproduced by kind permission of BP Educational Service

was not appropriate. Perhaps an absorption and collection method would be preferable. I was impressed by the group's attitudes and logical thought processes displayed while discussing these and similar problems before using the programs.

Two particular skills had to be acquired before the group could get to grips with the program. In order to combat a slick they had to learn how to estimate its position on the grid map, using wind speed and direction data. This was particularly important as unless a correct prediction was entered, no action against the slick such as loading up a tug with dispersant chemicals, placing booms, or even moving the tug was possible. As the time allowed for assessing slick movement was limited (one movement per every fifteen minutes, computer time, not actual time) the children had to be very quick in their predictions. Working in pairs with duplicated grid maps, each couple prepared a sample map on which the plotted co-ordinates of each of the slick's movements were shown. Each pair took new maps and tried tracing the courses of their friends' oil slicks from the co-ordinates given. The element of competition in this exercise was very high indeed and was equally evident as each of the other groups were introduced to the program in turn.

Excitement reached fever pitch as the group came to the micro to combat a 'real' slick for the first time. They were informed by a series of letters that they had been appointed Conservation Officers for the area of Northsands Bay and that they had inherited five thousand pounds worth of equipment and chemicals from the previous officer in readiness to combat an oil spillage should one occur. The program was then run for the first time using the inherited resources. I was pleased to observe the high number of correct predictions. The quality of decision making was very good and every member of the group assumed command and had to make final decisions at times of group indecision. This was a rule I made to ensure that every child had equal opportunity to contribute and command, rather than allow a natural leader to control the group to the exclusion of his less forceful and less able peers. The following week the group recorded details of their first effort in their log books and charted the slick on a definite map, then had a second try on the micro, this time choosing their own resources, spending up to the five thousand pounds allocated. Second and third groups were introduced to the program during the same lesson.

Micro time was fully allocated throughout the project. Both computers were available for data base work for the first few weeks, each of the six groups working for thirty minutes on one of the two machines. Following the introduction of *Slick*, the second micro allowed three groups to operate the program for thirty minutes each. It was purely fortuitous that one could in fact operate the program in full within a thirty-minute time span although there is a facility for the user to save his program to the point of stopping and re-loading it to continue at the same point at a later date.

I suggested that each group should display its slick and results in the

Figure 3

same way so that comparisons could be made. It became apparent to the children by making such comparisons that there was no one perfectly satisfactory method of combating oil slicks at sea and that much depended on the wise selection of resources to begin with.

Other areas investigated

Although about half of each group's presented project was based on traditional methods, that is general research of written and illustrated materials, the remainder of the work reflected the acquisition and employment of new skills. One group had used the bottled and labelled oil samples to conduct experiments such as which floated and which dispersed naturally in water. One girl brought in a can of engine grease and carefully organized experiments were conducted to see how difficult it was to use absorption and collection methods using materials such as straw and broken-up polystyrene ceiling tiles. The group that had conducted a local garage survey wondered why vehicles which used petrol were considerably greater in number than diesel powered vehicles when diesel fuel was always cheaper than any of the grades of petrol.

The group using *Inform* had collected an enormous amount of data about United Kingdom oil refinery production. The completed file was interrogated for many kinds of information. The most surprising was that no less than fourteen different companies had operated plants in the UK since 1921 and that the smallest had been operating in Dundee since 1935 and was still refining oil at a rate of 850 thousand tonnes per annum in 1982. The children and I were amazed to discover that a BP plant in Lothian was refining oil in the year 1884 and didn't close down until 1964! The group that produced the file were quick to point out that they had discovered that refining operations total output increased dramatically between 1965 and the present — a fact they attributed to the growth of the North Sea oil fields. One child in the group noticed that all the refineries were located at major ports or on major river estuaries. Her reasoning for this geographical phenomenon was that if they caught fire there was plenty of water available to put them out! She was upset when other members of the group had laughed at this suggestion but they accepted the logic of the deduction when I asked them to find another reason for siting plants in this type of location. The group prepared a ten question exercise for other groups to use with their database which everyone enjoyed.

The presentation

A group of five children who shared a particular interest in art were allowed eight pages of *Edfax* for their presentation as two of the other groups used only two pages out of their allocation and these were for title and contents type pages only. This group worked hard at producing a title and contents page as well but the other six pages were used to explain and show graphically some of the major uses of oil products from butane gas for camping to toiletries, car tyres and clothing. Everyone enjoyed looking at this presentation and some wished that they had worked harder at it.

Every group produced a booklet at the end of the term's work covering all the aspects of their work. One used cartoons as illustrations of their work and a couple of booklets contained 'letters home' from workers on an oil-rig. The letters were written by girls and as the basis of both letters was the hardship of living and working on a rig for two weeks at a time and how much they missed their wives and families, I wondered if the project was too boy-orientated from an interest point of view. I was somewhat relieved, however, to find that the girls had found the project enjoyable and interesting, particularly fighting oil spillages in the *Slick* program and preparing *Edfax* pages. Nevertheless, one or two said that they thought it was the sort of project that boys would like more than girls.

Advantage of using the micro

The principal differences in undertaking a project like this today instead of some years ago was that we were using high technology resources for the first time. Therefore our researches were more realistic than library books and pamphlets alone. The project related to everyday living and needs, from private transport and home heating costs to the simulation of controlling oil slicks. I believe that using the micro in this way helped to maintain children's interest throughout. Although one group became a little dispirited their interest was rekindled through *Slick*. As a class teacher in the past I had always been acutely aware that no matter how much time and energy I put into project work, I inevitably lost the interest of certain children somewhere along the way. It is significant that interest and application in respect of this project was sustained to the end, not as a result of my efforts, but because the approach appealed more to the children's sense of doing something in a more 'grown-up' way.

Without the micro the project would have been more pedestrian, particularly in data presentation, and the simulation exercise could not have been done in any other way. Children recognise the existence and uses of new technological resources when many adults are quite blind to them. The techniques of viewdata presentation and therefore of information handling skills such as data collection, interrogation and deduction will soon become commonplace in everyday life. Today's children will grow up with these skills and will have no fear of them.

I would have liked to have used a word-processing facility with the class but the time constraints operating obliged me to save this for a future project. I do believe that word-processing with the school micros is a marvellous facility. Creativity is all too often blunted by the process of writing. When a child can manipulate its own written work — editing, correcting errors and improving work — before justifying it and finally producing it in its printed form, the quality of work can be dramatically improved. Unless one has a Quinkey Microwriter facility (7), which enables four children to use one microcomputer as a word processor at the same time, the time constraints on the one or two micros a school might possess, make word processing a very difficult proposition indeed, particularly in connection with this kind of project work.

The potential of the micro used in the manner described is enormous but as yet relatively untapped. Many primary schools have only one micro and there are several constraints which often prevent good micro practice. Software acquisition is difficult — it is often expensive and virtually unexaminable before purchase. Peripherals such as disk drives and printers are desired, but beyond the purchasing power of most primaries. Staff training in using the micro is also very limited. Often only one or two members of staff have had the benefit of attending a beginners' course and just as often they return to school designated the 'experts' by staff unwilling to come to terms with the new technology themselves or unable to do so immediately. Microtechnology and computer usage in the primary school is still in its infancy of course and the support of the head is crucial in its development.

Role of the head

The head does not have to be the innovator, but he or she needs to be fully supportive of staff using the micro and should encourage other staff to explore its potential in their teaching. It would be an unwise head who delegated micro usage to another member of staff completely. An ostrich-like attitude of this kind is likely to kill any drive or initiative displayed by more open-minded teachers in the establishment. The head must learn with his or her staff, to maintain credibility if nothing else. Where LEAs lack sufficient funds to initiate courses in micro usage in the classroom, local schools would do well to set up local teacher groups to exchange ideas about software and classroom micro experience. This is one of the best ways of passing on good practice and ought to be encouraged.

Challenge of the micro

The argument that using a micro in the classroom has not proved itself to be of positive value to both the pupils and the teacher has validity only because the majority of teachers are inexperienced in its use — it is still very early days indeed. The fact is that our pupils accept and welcome this new technology much more readily than we adults do. We live in a world of high technology which sees new uses and advances every day. We owe it to our pupils to meet the challenges presented and to take advantage of all that such technology can offer. If nothing else was achieved by using micros in the project, the stimulus of using them maintained the interest of the pupils throughout a lengthy term. I believe the aims of the project were achieved by this approach and I know the children enjoyed learning in this 'grown-up' way.

7

Managing innovation: results of an investigation

The previous chapters have described innovation in one classroom rather than in a whole school. But if information skills teaching or any other curriculum development is to be completely successful, it must have the support of the head, a committed staff, and a supporting organizational framework. Teachers need time to discuss and compare their ideas, and establish ways of co-operating so that children progressing through school can practise and reinforce developing skills from one year to the next. They also need an opportunity to compare notes on resources used in the school, to create their own if necessary, and to agree a policy on the organization of the library and resource area.

Marion Griffin's investigation, commissioned by the British Library and NFER, looks at eight schools. Five had been identified as implementing study or information skills teaching, three, as a comparison, were included because they made no claims to be teaching these skills. Curriculum innovation is never easy to sustain across a whole school and two of the five schools where information skills had been introduced had now ceased to include them in the curriculum. Since Marion's research was limited by time and the smallness of the sample it is difficult to draw too many rigid conclusions, but this brief look at such schools highlights the difficulty of introducing change. It suggests that a committed individual can succeed in producing change, but it appears to last only if colleagues fully understand the nature of the change and commit themselves to it also. Without this, it can fade away if the instigator leaves the school.

It is also important that teachers are aware of new thinking in areas such as information skills, so it is important that information channels are created. Heads and advisers can play an important role in disseminating new ideas and organizing INSET courses.

At best, educational research should help to highlight ways in which the content of classroom teaching might be improved, particularly by examining what is good practice. The chapter includes as an appendix details of recent research in the area of information skills teaching and indicates where further information or published work can be obtained.

7

Managing innovation: results of an investigation

Marion Griffin

During the course of the joint British Library and NFER sponsored project, *Study and Information Skills in Schools* (1), contacts had been made with a number of primary schools where some form of innovative practice in the teaching of study and information skills was taking place. An interest in why and how innovation had been attempted in these schools and the teaching practices developed led to the commissioning of an investigation and report in the spring of 1983 (2). It was felt that an understanding of the experiences of a few teachers who had been success-ful in developing and implementing new ideas might prove helpful to others attempting change. In addition, the information gained would be useful in identifying areas where further research and development was needed.

The short duration of the research, a total of six weeks to cover the collection and analysis of data and completion of a report, inevitably limited the number of schools that could be visited and the amount of time spent in each school. Eight schools were included in the study: five of these being schools where innovation was known to have taken place. The other three schools had no specific innovatory work going on and were included to highlight what was being done in general practice to encourage children's independent learning.

One day was spent in each school, making classroom observations and talking to teachers. As problems of terminology had been foreseen, the research brief was presented to schools in terms of an interest in 'how children find and use information'.

The sample schools

Seven schools in the study were in urban areas and one was in a rural setting. Of these, five were county junior schools (7—11 years); two were mixed infants and juniors (5—11 years), and one was a first school (5—9 years). Three of the sample schools were in designated 'special priority areas'.

Details of administration and organization were gathered in each school to provide a background for the practices observed. It was possible to appreciate those areas that were particularly influential in determining a school's environment and opportunities for innovation. It was also possible to appreciate from even the small number of schools contained in the sample, the extent to which schools differ in terms of organization.

Main areas of influence

Grouping of children, classroom and curriculum organization
Children could be grouped in single year age groups or mixed year age groups. Classroom organization was primarily the responsibility of the class teacher. However, in some schools an agreed approach had been adopted throughout the school, for example, the integrated day. This was particularly the case in schools where some form of innovative practice or 'whole-school' policy had been established. In fact, in seven of the eight schools there were explicit guidelines for various areas of the curriculum which determined a defined timetable of activities for the classroom.

Attitude of headteacher
The amount of teacher independence and direction from the headteacher varied considerably between schools. However, 'direction' was not necessarily at the expense of 'democracy'. Where the influence of the headteacher appeared to be considerable, it was still possible for an organizational structure to exist which included staff involvement and decision-making at most levels.

Headteachers encouraged members of their staff to attend courses and bring back what they had learned to benefit the school. Some headteachers expressed scepticism about any form of innovation being possible at a time of staff cutbacks. Others took the opposite view, that it was even more important in a time of austerity to look at current practices to assess their real worth.

Staff discussion
Teachers' family commitments were said to make after-school meetings impossible in some schools. In others, regular seminars were held after school. One headteacher took whole-school assembly once a week so that his staff could meet within the school day. In most schools, curriculum planning was carried out through whole-staff discussion.

Staffing levels and parental involvement
Falling rolls and staff cuts were affecting most schools, the number of part-time teaching posts and peripatetic staff being severely reduced. Inevitably, the effect on a school was a reduction in teaching time as teachers were obliged to carry out responsibilities previously taken care of by support staff. Understandably, in this situation some teachers felt

unable to attempt anything new. However, it was seen that the amount of parental help given to a school could be considerable and this assistance supported the introduction of innovatory ideas. Parents assisted in the running of school libraries, organized book clubs and became involved in children's reading.

Books and other resources

Although there were some obviously proven and popular materials in evidence in nearly every school, there were also many differences between schools in the materials used for language development programmes, reading and work schemes. Most schools used a number of reading schemes, and many used a system of correlating the material contained within different schemes by reading level. This gave children variety in their reading by being able to progress from one ability level to another within a number of different schemes.

Some reading schemes had associated workcards to develop particular language skills. The development of language skills was also built into a variety of different work schemes and language laboratories, and several included the development of specific information and study skills in the exercises provided.

Additional resources in schools included a variety of books (non-fiction and fiction), televisions, video recorders, projectors, and computers. Some teachers expressed doubts as to the usefulness of the computer as another education 'tool', however, many teachers were currently taking computer courses and hoped to have some of their doubts resolved. The potential of the computer in encouraging children's independent learning was acknowledged, but considered an area where further development was needed.

Positioning of resources

The availability of resources was an important factor in looking at how children went about finding and using information. Some schools had central resource areas and it was common practice for books to be made available both within classrooms or teaching areas and in the library. All libraries were described as being 'open' throughout the school day. However, the organization of children's time was seen to limit the opportunities for them to use the library. Another factor in the library's use was its proximity to the classroom. The books seen in classrooms were usually a good mixture of non-fiction reference material and a variety of fiction in the reading schemes used.

Classification systems in libraries could be by colour coding of subject matter, or by the Dewey Decimal System. These systems were usually explained to the children by their class teacher, but in some schools it was done by the headteacher or the teacher with responsibility for the library.

Outside support and in-service training

In general, outside support was considered to be good. Local library services assisted schools in the development and classification of their libraries, often producing guidelines for the development of children's library skills. A variety of courses were provided by local teachers' centres with an INSET representative appointed in most schools. Local authority advisers were felt to be active and supportive, particularly in the development of in-service training, working closely with teachers' centres, local universities, institutes of education and training colleges. In all the schools, teachers felt constrained to take up some form of full time in-service training, because supply cover was no longer available. Release was only possible through reorganization within the school. The attitude of an authority was seen to be very influential in the amount and type of in-service training opportunities made available to teachers; both through the types of courses offered and the amount of co-operation encouraged between schools.

A number of teachers expressed the view that in the dissemination of information across schools, more was to be gained from spending time in each other's schools than in attending courses. If, however, dissemination was attempted through in-service courses, then whole-school involvement, or that of at least a number of staff, *and* the commitment of the head-teacher was desirable. This approach should at least make it easier for changes to be *attempted* in a school, rather than by an individual trying to act alone.

Observed practices

On visiting the five schools where it was known some form of innovation of information skills' teaching had been attempted, it was learned, in fact, that only three had been successful. In these schools, the original ideas introduced had been developed and continued. In the remaining two schools, the attempted innovation had not been sustained.

To consider the factors that contributed to the success, or failure, of innovation, the information gathered in each school is presented within a common format:

> How and why innovation started (or was attempted)
> Nature of innovation and age of children involved (or where innovation had failed, current skills' teaching practices)
> Materials and resources used
> Teaching methods
> Teachers' assessment of value of practices

Three examples of successful innovation

In schools, A, B and C three very different forms of innovation had been attempted and proved successful.

School A (junior school 7—11; 315 on roll; 10 full-time staff)

How and why innovation started
The staff in the school felt that the children were ill-prepared to cope with some of the tasks set within topic work. To meet this need, and through his own interest and expertise, a former language adviser had developed a range of 'research skills' exercises.

Nature of innovation and age of children involved
The 'research skills' exercises were contained in two booklets according to difficulty, and covered a wide range of ability from simple alphabetical tasks to sophisticated diagram and graph comprehension.

Materials and resources used
The skills exercises were designed to complement the regular topic work carried out throughout the school. Two different topics ran parallel through the lower and upper school each term, the children being vertically grouped in mixed first and second year classes (7—9 year olds), and third and fourth years (9—11 years old).

Some of the 'research skills' exercises depended upon the use of other material and resources, for example, alphabet letter pieces (for alphabetical order games), specific encyclopaedias, dictionaries, spelling books and other textbooks in general use throughout the school. At the beginning of an exercise children could be asked to turn to a specified page in an encyclopedia and complete a particular task from the information given there.

Teaching methods
An integrated day was practised throughout the school. In one of the classrooms visited, a grid was written up on the blackboard indicating the four areas of work to be covered during the day: class topic (school topic); mathematics; research skills; own topic (children's choice). The grid also showed how these areas were to be divided up between the four groups of children in the class, that is, groups A to D. The day was divided into four periods, before and after break, a.m. and p.m. A diagram of the grid is shown in Figure 1.

The teacher worked with each group as a whole, or with individual children, the 'research skills' exercises being worked through by the children on their own. Reference books were available in the class and the library could be visited at any time. The library was run by parents on a rota system, so an adult was always present to help the children.

Teachers' assessment of the value of practices
After nearly a year in operation, teachers felt the 'research skills' exercises were very valuable. The fact that children could work at them on their

A	OT	RS	M	CT
B	RS	M	CT	OT
C	M	CT	OT	RS
D	CT	OT	RS	M

OT — own topic

RS — research skills

M — mathematics

CT — class topic (school theme)

Figure 1

own made it easy to incorporate them into the classroom organization — an important design feature. The fact that both the skills exercises and topic work could be built into the school's integrated day meant that the children could have daily exposure to the exercises and daily opportunities to apply the skills they had learned.

School B (junior school 7—11; 228 on school roll; 7 full-time staff)

How and why innovation started

The headteacher's early teaching experience had been with adults who had been so 'disabled' as he put it, by their school experiences that they were under-achieving academically and held themselves in poor esteem. Developing their abilities to organize their own learning improved their self-esteem and, in turn, extended their learning strategies. The outcome was that their academic achievements improved as they developed a more realistic understanding of their own competence.

From this background the head's overall philosophy had evolved. He had been in the school since it opened six years previously, so from the start he was able to introduce his ideas for the staff to consider. Through their co-operation, initial ideas had been developed into current practices.

Nature of innovation and age of children involved

A range of learning-to-learn procedures had been developed within a philosophy that children should be involved with the development of their own learning: they should be encouraged to evaluate and review their own learning processes and, through an appreciation of this learning, develop strategies to become more efficient learners. This philosophy was applied to everything that went on in the school, involving all staff and children and across all curriculum areas.

Materials and resources used

Learning procedures and techniques had been developed rather than actual materials. It was therefore process-based, the procedures devised operating at three levels:

1) Techniques aimed at supporting the subject content of school tasks, by developing children's awareness of *how* they learn, i.e. the actual processes involved.
2) Formal review where, through the use of special review forms, teachers, parents, the children themselves and their peers could comment in a structured way on performance outcomes and identify future needs.
3) Informal review and reworking of the learning experiences that had been found to be successful, e.g. by describing how a correct solution had been obtained and giving an analysis of why this was so.

Teaching methods

As in other schools, topic work was one vehicle through which the procedures were learned. For example, in a class of eleven year olds, the children were working on a topic about a nearby village, which they had recently visited. In describing this visit, the children set down the main points, (i.e. what they did and what they saw), as a skeletal diagram. From this they could see how factors could be grouped into related units of meaning, i.e. sentences, paragraphs, sections. It was also possible to see how initial factors, or points, could lead to others in developing branches from the main skeleton.

Another strategy was for the children to look in detail at the words they had used in their first drafts. Within a 'writing analysis' exercise, words were grouped in a variety of different ways. One example was by the number of letters and syllables they contained. From this children could see the amount of repetition that existed in their draft texts and select more appropriate alternative words for the final description. Children worked at their own speed through these exercises, which were often self-chosen.

Regular reviews of children's progress and future needs enabled frequent teacher/child discussion and provided a review of overall progress achieved through the term. A summary of termly reviews covered a child's progress through the school, and were incorporated into a final review of primary experience on transfer to the secondary school.

Teachers' assessment of the value of practices

Initially, regular standardized testing had been carried out, for the staff to be certain that the children were acquiring basic knowledge through the learning techniques used. Testing was now carried out very infrequently, the school being confident that the effectiveness of their methods and the underlying principles were producing the changes expected in the children. They could demonstrate in their ordinary classroom performances the effects of their learning activities.

School C (junior school 7–11; 216 on roll; 9 full-time staff)

How and why innovation started
Innovation grew out of an experiment carried out in a class of eight and nine year olds, by the headteacher and another member of staff. The initiative came from the head, arising out of an interest in children's language development and reading.

Nature of innovation and age of children involved
The focus of the initial experiment was on developing children's note-taking skills. The ideas generated were considered so valuable by other staff members that the strategies were developed and adopted throughout the school. They covered all areas of the curriculum and age-groups.

Materials and resources used
Written guidelines for developing notetaking skills had been produced, giving teachers an indication of the areas of sub-skills that would be appropriate for different age-groups of children, for example listening skills, through an appreciation of the sequence of a story from comic strips for first year children and skimming and scanning techniques and evaluation of facts obtained from different sources for third and fourth years.

Guidelines had also been produced in a number of other areas, for example, reference skills – listing in alphabetical order using an index etc; study skills – listing main events in order, making inferences from a text; and evaluation skills – differentiating between fact, fiction and opinion, and checking the accuracy of information with that from another source.

A 'study skills' checklist had also been prepared to be used once or twice a term. These materials, together with a range of 'reading and investigation' exercises were used in conjunction with the books and other resources available in the classrooms and school library.

Teaching methods
An integrated-day system of classroom organization operated throughout the school. In one class visited, (seven year olds), the activities for the day were written up on the blackboard and covered five areas. The first was a story about either a fairy or giant (a comprehension exercise being completed from the previous day. The children had been read a poem about a fairy and told a story about a giant and were now writing their own account). The second activity was drawing story pictures (after hearing the story of Cinderella, children were making their own picture

stories, i.e. drawing the main points of the story in the correct sequence. The third was a craft activity (printing with string and paint) and the fourth was topic work (the five senses were being covered, and with 'Touch' the children were examining objects, writing down their names and words to describe how they felt). The fifth activity was practice in alphabetical order (putting words generated by earlier exercises into alphabetical order. Children were free to choose the order in which they completed the day's work activities, the teacher working with children individually.

In another class of mixed seven and eight year olds, the teacher had recently been on a course concerned with 'Approaches to Literature'. She had brought back an exercise introduced on the course to use with her children. This was to listen to a story and to ask, rather than answer, questions about it. As observed, a small group of children were sitting listening to a story on the tape recorder, each child having a set of head-phones and following the story in a book. The teacher explained that this freed her to work with other children and helped even the slow readers in their being able to follow the words as the story was being read. After the story was finished, the children, as a group, asked the teacher questions about what they had heard. It was felt that thinking about what questions to ask stimulated better comprehension of the story. Twenty stories had been taped to be used in this way.

Teachers' assessment of the value of practices
The headteacher said it was difficult to 'prove' the value of what they were doing but he considered the value was apparent in the commitment of the staff and the obvious 'growth' of the children. The children displayed their growth in the confidence with which they set about tasks, their competence when using the library and other resources, and in their general ability to discuss what they were doing and express their feelings. The views of the head were echoed in the comments of other teachers in the school.

Attempted but unsuccessful innovation

The circumstances in two schools where innovation had not been sustained are described in the details of schools D and E.

School D (mixed infants and juniors 5—11; 193 on roll; 8 full-time staff)

How and why innovation was attempted
The original idea had been that of the deputy headteacher who had developed study skills materials as part of an advanced diploma course. He had left the school about two years previously and there seemed to be no evidence of anything he had attempted currently being practised. The

headteacher and other members of staff seemed unsure of exactly what had been attempted. Certainly, no whole-school commitment was achieved. This may have been because:

a) the innovation was not considered of value by the other teachers;
b) the initiating member of staff did not 'sell' his ideas well or involve other teachers in their development;
c) the attitude of the headteacher may have been negative and influenced the attitudes of other staff;
d) the organization of the staff did not lend itself to general discussion about possible innovation, whereby a 'whole-school' policy might be adopted.

Current skills teaching practices and age of children involved

There was no 'whole-school' policy in respect of curriculum planning and classroom organization. Class teachers worked independently within the syllabus and children were grouped in single year age groups. In general, they worked as individual units with only a limited amount of co-operative activity. During the day's visit, no specific skills teaching was observed, although children were seen using the library.

Materials and resources used

There was a very well stocked library situated in the centre of the school. It had recently been reorganized and reclassified with the help of the local library service. Eleven year old pupils were observed using the library. They were obviously familiar with the Dewey Decimal classification system and were using the library to complete projects.

Teaching methods

No specific skills teaching was observed, but the headteacher and other members of staff said children were encouraged to develop independent learning skills and to find out things for themselves. The headteacher explained that, since the reorganization of the library, he had started taking groups of top infant children into the library to teach them the classification system and what was involved in using books.

General classroom practices observed: whole class answering the teacher's questions about a television programme seen earlier; children working individually through language comprehension exercises; and two classes in adjacent rooms engaged in co-operative work on a project.

Teachers' assessment of the value of practices

Some teachers felt that children were acquiring learning skills through their normal classroom work, while others believed that more could be done if a structured approach was developed throughout the school. There was some doubt expressed about whether this would be likely, owing to differences of opinion known to exist about the value of such an exercise. These differences may have arisen when innovation was attempted.

School E (junior school 7—11; 220 on roll; 9 full-time staff)

How and why innovation was attempted
The innovation attempted had been through the former headteacher's desire to incorporate into the school's curriculum the teaching of study skills. Although many of the ideas were valuable, the organizational factors surrounding them proved unworkable. The 'child-centred' practices involved the children following and developing their own interests within broad subject channels, for example communication, biological studies, and transport. With the children vertically grouped and in mixed ability classes, the teachers had the almost impossible task of organizing what were, in effect, thirty different activities.

Current skills teaching practices and age of children involved
The present headteacher had introduced many of the present practices into the school and explained that his own experiences had convinced him of the value of children acquiring independent learning skills. His ideas had been introduced gradually as he described the staff as 'change-contaminated' and understandably sceptical about new ideas.

The school's curriculum was divided into three broad areas: maths, language development, and project work, across all age-groups of children. Within project work guidelines, attention was given to the development of a variety of study skills: use of index; skimming and scanning; the sequencing of facts; note-taking, and so on. Children were in single year age-groups, with two parallel classes working together on the same project. This provided mutual support for the two class teachers and allowed co-operative work and the sharing of 'project-pack' materials and museum artefacts on loan. Each child's individual pieces of project work were collected throughout the term and bound together to produce a project folder. The children were made aware of the need for items to be presented in a logical order, for there to be variety in the written and illustrative work included, and for titles, contents and other information to be clear and easy to read.

Materials and resources used
No specific materials were used but, in the guidelines for the development of study skills, the policy was to have children use all the available resources in the school. The school had two libraries (fiction and non-fiction), and a central resource area.

Teaching methods
There was no set policy regarding classroom organization, teachers being

free to divide their working day as they wished within the three curriculum areas.

In the classes observed, children were working on their projects, engaged in creative writing and illustrating. Two first year classes were working together on a new project 'Our Homes'. From the children's suggestions a list of characteristics (environment, family, pets, furniture and so on) were being written up on the blackboard. This list would be discussed later for the children to see how factors could be grouped and ordered in the production of their folders. Within project work strategy, the importance of linking themes close to pupils' experiences was considered essential. For example, first year children would work on such themes as their homes, parks, or the postman.

Teachers' assessment of the value of practices
The teachers felt that their overall teaching approach was a valuable one. Projects were considered to be a flexible medium, allowing the individual interests of both children and teachers to be explored, but contained within a defined structure and purpose. The production of a final project folder was felt to reinforce children's appreciation of what was involved in presenting the information contained in a book.

Common practice

The last three schools in the sample were schools where, so far as it was known, no particular study and information skills teaching was being practised. The observations made in these schools are summarized below.

Within the work scheme and language laboratories available in the schools, a considerable amount of teaching of specific learning skills was observed. This teaching was incorporated into a school's language development programme, project or topic work.

Teaching methods
Classroom organization in the three schools was:

    a) team teaching within an integrated day;
    b) single year age-groups operating the integrated day;
    c) a mixture of single year age-groups and mixed year age-groups working independently within their own classroom organization.

The teachers working the integrated day felt this made it easier for children to move around freely, using the books and other resources available, and allowed a teacher to give time to an individual child knowing the others in the class were occupied.

In each school the library was 'open' throughout the day and had a defined classification system. Use of the library was said to be taught to children early in the junior school.

Observed activities involving children's use of learning skills included:

1) A group of eleven year olds working independently through the exercises contained in a language laboratory, involving the use of dictionaries.

2) A class of eleven year olds re-writing in their own words a passage from a reference book on their topic subject. There was no interim note-taking stage, the descriptions being written straight on to the final sheet. The class teacher explained that the children had worked through the stage where a first draft was necessary.

3) Another group of eleven year olds were writing their own television scripts. This required them to demonstrate their proficiency in a number of independent learning skills: choosing a suitable subject, finding the information required, and presenting it in a logical sequence in a piece of interesting writing.

Teachers' assessment of the value of practices

The general view expressed by teachers was that the teaching of skills needed to be incorporated into the actual tasks children were set. Children needed to see the relevance and usefulness of the skills they had acquired. Some work schemes and language kits available were considered very good, with the exercises they contained covering a wide range of ability levels. The fact that they were designed so that children could work through them at their own speed made it easier for them to be incorporated into the classroom. A similar view was expressed by staff in School A with reference to their 'research skills' exercises.

Like staff in some of the other schools visited, several teachers commented on the need for a 'whole-school' policy in the teaching of study skills. Individual classroom practices were valuable, but a policy consistent throughout the school gave children continuity of experience and enabled staff to reinforce skills that had been learned before.

Reflections and conclusions

The purpose of the research was to look at how the teaching of study and information skills had been attempted in a few primary schools, what opportunities existed for innovation, and what constraints operated. The opportunities that existed in the schools where innovation had been possible can be identified as certain common and contributory factors and summarized under three headings.

How and why innovation started

Innovation was initially the idea of one person who had the interest and expertise to develop materials and/or strategies in response to an identified area of need.

How innovation was made possible

This was usually through the positive attitude of the headteacher; the 'democracy' of the school and existence of 'whole-school' policy; staff willingness to work on materials in their own time; the availability of resources (either appropriate existing materials or the financial means to develop new ones); support from outside agencies in the help given by advisers, teachers' centres and library services.

How innovation was sustained and developed

This was usually by continuing staff commitment based on the considered value of the practice and the ease with which it could be integrated into other classroom activities; the flexibility of the innovation — teachers feeling they were in control of the practice, not the other way round; opportunities for in-service training to allow ideas to be discussed with others, reinforcing teachers' own sense of value and personal contribution.

Constraints

In considering opportunities in general for teachers to attempt innovation, the enquiry revealed a number of constraints. There would seem to be little opportunity for teachers to: a) become aware of what can be done to develop children's learning skills without the initiative and expertise of an individual member of staff; b) learn about the range of materials available to help the teaching of skills (although a wealth exists); c) examine materials to assess their appropriateness for their own needs; d) learn about the innovations of others, within often limited school liaison procedures.

Staffing cuts, lack of financial resources, and the limitations of old buildings were other constraints identified. A constraint put forward by a number of teachers was that the 'dragging' effect on a class of a large number of children with low levels of ability would limit what could be attempted. It would be unrealistic to try to develop independent learning skills with children who could not read or write, although the needs of these children were even greater. Finally, several headteachers drew attention to what was not a constraint on practice within the primary school, but a break in the continuity of children's education, namely, that little or no reinforcement was given to children's primary practices once they entered the secondary school.

Future research

The main issue to arise from this study must be whether the children in the schools where innovatory ideas were being practised were gaining something more or better than the children in other primary schools. The teachers involved considered the practices valuable in terms of the positive attitudes and self-confidence of the children.

The secondary interest of the research was to identify areas where further research and development would be valuable. One possibility would be a study of current innovatory practices, paying greater attention than has been possible in this enquiry to the outcomes of innovation. From the concerns expressed by teachers, it would be beneficial to include examples of programmes developed for the less able and/or very young.

The other area where further research would be valuable is the dissemination of information to teachers. Increased opportunities are needed for teachers to:

1) appreciate the importance of developing children's learning skills (e.g. through relevant research);
2) be informed about the range of materials that exist in order for them to be able to select those appropriate for their own use;
3) learn from the experiences of others.

Local authority advisers, teachers' centres, and headteachers are the main agencies through which information is channelled to teachers. Ways need to be explored of how these channels can be widened for teachers to benefit from research findings and the innovatory practices of others. The headteacher has been seen as a key figure in successful innovation and therefore a crucial target for the dissemination of information. A view expressed by teachers when discussing in-service training was that the commitment of the head was essential and, ideally, the involvement of a whole school or at least that of a number of staff.

Evaluative descriptions of teaching materials could be made available on computer, and centres already making certain materials available for inspection might be able to extend this provision. To enable teachers to see materials in use, increased school liaison would be valuable. The value of spending time in each other's schools was a view expressed by several teachers in the research.

Finally, since topic work appears to be the medium through which children exercise the skills they have learned, ways could be explored of developing topic work to reinforce the teaching of skills and encourage the transfer of newly-learned techniques.

Disclaimer   Although this was a sponsored project, it should be noted that the views expressed in this account are solely those of the author.

Appendix

Related research

The findings of this brief study suggest some areas where further research would be valuable. These need to be considered in relation to the exploratory work of others in the field.

The relevance of classroom organization, children's language development and topic work to the teaching of study skills at the primary level has been demonstrated in this research. In the design of the 'research skills' exercises in school A, the value of children being able to work independently, and the dovetailing of the exercises with topic work were appreciated by the teachers.

A description of the organization of the primary classroom was given in the research of Galton, Simon and Croll (3) and the division of pupils' time across the curriculum and the development of topic work were two areas investigated by the NFER project *Nine Hundred Primary School Teachers* (4). Both pieces of research illustrated the need for a review of current opportunities for children to develop independent learning skills.

The practices described have shown how the teaching of skills can be incorporated into children's language development and encouraged through topic work. The learning-to-learn procedures and strategies adopted in schools B and C were designed to be incorporated into topic work. Similarly, the relevance of the study skills they were acquiring to the tasks involved in their project work was made apparent to the children in school E.

The teaching of skills within language programmes and topic work has been the focus of further research (5), and a variety of innovative practices has been attempted in schools. The current 'Study and Information Skills' project at the NFER has information about several programmes and is looking in detail at how some examples of innovation have been implemented.

Three other investigations which focus on study and information skills teaching deserve mention.

The work of Rosemary Webb looked at the following issues: teachers' understandings of the nature and role of information skills and the opportunities for information-handling that these methods provide; children's definitions and perceptions of information and its location; and the problems faced by children in developing information skills. Within the research an attempt was made to develop, implement and evaluate materials and strategies for teaching information skills (6).

Pauline Heather's research looked into information skills teaching and how this is followed up by pupils in their own independent projects. Teaching methods were examined, as well as children's investigation practices. This enabled a comparison to be made of their performance in skills teaching lessons and when conducting their own project work (7).

Pat Avann's work in Coventry combined action research with opportunities for in-service training. The findings from her research formed the basis of an in-service course, allowing the research information to be disseminated and enabling practising teachers to discuss and comment on what had been attempted. The main focus of the research was on children's topic work and how it was linked to ways of encouraging the development of reference skills (8).

8

Summing up

Pat Avann

This book set out to attempt to provide some ideas for teaching information skills. Perhaps the reader will experience some feeling of disappointment that this has not resulted in an explanation of how skills can be taught as a 'subject', but of how they have been taught through topic work, problem solving, and so on. The essence of information skills is that they are, or should be, used in the day-to-day work of the classroom. Such skills underpin all subject work and should not be isolated from other areas of the curriculum. It is important to be able to recognize their existence and be able to define individual skills. If necessary, a *short* time can be spent in practising some of them as exercises. But the message of this book is to plan topic or other work recognizing that such skills are an integral part of that work and of equal importance with the content.

The inclusion of information skills in this way needs careful planning by teachers and the adoption of a role as creator of learning opportunities, supporting the children, especially those with learning difficulties, but not leading them.

Education and training

This may present a challenge to some teachers since it is necessary sometimes to say

'I don't know the answer to that question, but I can help you to find out for yourself'.

This assumes that teachers already have information skills, but their own education and training may not have included finding out for oneself very effectively either. Evidence from the LASS project on sixth form study (1) indicates that sixth formers in many schools do not have any practice in independent learning despite a lip service to the idea of autonomy at this level of schooling. If we feel that many children fail to develop information skills as part of their education, there is no reason to suppose that their teachers have done so either.

Even if the skills are there, they may not have been recognized and defined so that they can be passed on to the children.

Teachers can be helped to do this by INSET, either through the LEA advisers, courses in teacher education institutions or in individual schools.

I believe too, that successful information skills teaching should begin in the infant schools. This needs not only an agreed policy for a particular school, but discussion between different levels of schools in a particular locality.

Assessment

One difficulty that teachers experience when teaching information skills is how to discover what the children have learnt. Because the skills are pervasive, it can be difficult to assess progress. One solution is to use checklists which list various skills and there are some examples in the preceding chapters. However, too long a list of what may be felt to be sometimes nebulous skills can be difficult to cope with in a busy teacher's day. Perhaps it may be sufficient to rely on observations that children do appear to be more confident in their use of the library, more critical of the content of information sources, that their written work relies less on copying from books or that they can present a balanced and reasoned argument in a class discussion.

In conclusion

Learning to be a learner is too important to be left to chance and the school has an important contribution to make to the development of effective, flexible, independent learners. Therefore, this contribution should be planned as part of the curriculum and cannot begin too early in the child's school life.

References

Introduction

1 Galton, M., Simon, B. and Croll, P. *Inside the Primary Classroom*, RKP, 1980.
2 Rudduck, Jean and Hopkins, David, *The sixth form and libraries: problems of access to knowledge*, (Library and Information Research Report, 24), British Library Board, 1984.
3 Southgate, V., Arnold, H. and Johnson, S. *Extending Beginning Reading*, (Schools Council Project), Heinemann Educational, 1981.
4 Cooper, John, *Directions*, Oliver and Boyd, 1978—82 (currently seven books in this series).
5 *SRA Research Lab*, Henley-on-Thames, Science Research Associates, Inc., 1974.
6 Marland, Michael (ed.), *Information skills in the secondary curriculum: the recommendations of a working group sponsored by the British Library and the Schools Council*, (Schools Council Curriculum Bulletin 9), Methuen Educational, 1981.
7 Irving, Ann (ed.), *Starting to Teach Study Skills* (Teaching Matters), Edward Arnold, 1982.

Chapter 3

1 DES, *Special Educational Needs*, London, HMSO, 1978.
2 DES, *Primary Education in England*, London, HMSO, 1978.
3 Southgate, V., Arnold, H. and Johnson, S. *Extending Beginning Reading*, (Schools Council Project) Heinemann Educational, 1981.
4 Tabberer, R. 'Linking Research and Practice' in Irving, A. (ed.) *Starting to Teach Study Skills*, London, Edward Arnold, 1982, pp 7—14.
5 Reid, J. 'Learning to Think About Reading' in *Educational Research*, 1966, pp 56—62.
6 Downing, J. *Reading and Reasoning*, Chambers, 1979.
7 Downing, J. 'The Theoretical and Research Basis' in Brown, A.L., Downing, J. and Soeats, J. *Words Children want to Use*, Chambers, 1971, pp 37—52.
8 Monroe, M. and Cabell, G. My Second Pictionary, Scott Foresman, Illinois, 1964.
9 DES, *Education 5—9: An illustrative survey of 80 first schools in England*, HMSO, 1982.

Chapter 4

1 Unstead, R. J. *Looking at History, Book 1: From Cavemen to Vikings*, A & C Black, 1974.
2 Gorman, T. P. (and others) *Language Performance in Schools*, Assessment of Performance Unit (Primary Survey Report No. 1), HMSO, 1981.
3 *Richmond Tests of Basic Skills* (levels 1—6), Nelson, 1975.

4 Bennett, Neville (and others) *Teaching Styles and Pupils' Progress*, Open Books, 1976.
5 Schools Council Project: *Developing Children's Thinking Through Topic Work*, School of Education, University of Nottingham, Project Co-ordinator Trevor Kerry, (in progress).

Chapter 5

1 Kilpatrick, W. H. 'A Project Curriculum', in *Curriculum Design*, ed. Golby, M. *et al*. Open University Press, 1975.
2 Bullock, Sir A. *A Language For Life*, HMSO, 1975.
3 Schools Council, *Mixed-ability teaaching in mathematics*, Evans Methuen, 1977.
4 Dewey, J., *Democracy and Education*, Macmillan, 1916.
5 Do Bono, Edward, *Children Solve Problems*, Penguin, 1972.
6 *Open University PME 233 Course*, Open University Press, 1979.
7 Youngman, M. B. *Conducting and Analysing Questionnaires, Rediguide 12, TRC* — Rediguides Ltd., 1978.
8 Wheeler, D. K. *Curriculum Process*, University London Press, 1967.
9 Rae, G. and McPhillimy, W. N. *Learning in the Primary School, a systematic approach*, Hodder and Stoughton, 1976.
10 Kelly, A.V. *The Curriculum: Theory and Practice*, Harper and Row Publications, 1982.

Chapter 6

1 The Microelectronics Project's network of regional centres supports the development of computer skills in schools. An important part of this is their concern with INSET. Contact MEP, Cheviot House, Coach Lane Campus, Newcastle-upon-Tyne.
2 *Slick*, a simulation, produced by BP Educational Service, PO Box 5, Wetherby, West Yorkshire, LS23 7EH. Cassette and disk versions BBC Model B.
3 *Factfile*, an information handling package, produced by Cambridge Microsoftware, Cambridge University Press, The Edinburgh Building, Shaftesbury Road, Cambridge, CB2 2RU. Cassette version for BBC Model B, RML 480Z and Sinclair 48K.
4 *Inform*, an information handling package, produced by Nottinghamshire CC Education Dept., Computer Education Centre, Eaton Hall International, Retford, Notts, DN22 0PQ. Disk version for BBC Model B.
5 *Edfax*, a Teletext emulator, produced by Tecmedia Ltd, 5 Granby Street, Loughborough, Leicestershire, LE11 3DU. Disk only, BBC Model B.
6 *Wordworm*, a spelling game, produced by ITMA (Investigations on Teaching with Microcomputers as an Aid, Longman Primary catalogue, Longman Group Ltd (PSD), Fourth Avenue, Harlow, Essex. The above is for BBC Model B + RML 480Z. Note program is one of a pack of four programs — 'Module 1'.
7 *Quinkey Microwriter* is produced by Microwriter Ltd, Vector Marketing, Denington Estate, Wellingborough, Northants, NN8 2RL.

Chapter 7

1 *Study and Information Skills in Schools*, current British Library/National Foundation for Educational Research sponsored project. Completion date, June 1985.
2 Griffin, M. *Study and Information Skills in the Primary School*, British Library R & D Report 5784, 1983.
3 Galton M., Simon, B., and Croll, P., *op. cit.*

4   Bassey, M. *Nine Hundred Primary School Teachers*, Slough, National Foundation for Educational Research, 1981.

5   *Developing Pupils' Thinking Through Topic Work*, Schools Council project, *op. cit.*

6   Heather, Pauline, *A study of the use of books and libraries by children in primary schools* (CRUS occasional paper, 11). Sheffield Centre for Research on User Studies, 1984.

7   Webb, Rosemary, *School knowledge, pedagogy and development*, (an investigation into information skills in topic work centred on the primary and middle years), Norwich, University of East Anglia. Research in progress for a Ph.D thesis. Projected publication winter 1985.

8   Avann, Pat, *Information skills in primary schools: an investigation* . . . Loughborough University of Technology, 1983, (unpublished thesis).

Chapter 8

1   Rudduck, Jean, *op. cit.*

Bibliography

Avann, Pat, *Information skills in primary schools: an investigation . . .* Loughborough University of Technology, 1983, (unpublished thesis).

De Bono, Edward, *Children Solve Problems*, Penguin, 1972.

Committee of Inquiry into Reading and the Use of Language, *A Language for Life*: report of the Committee of Inquiry appointed by the Secretary of State for Education and Science under the chairmanship of Sir Alan Bullock, HMSO, 1975.

DES HM Inspectorate, *Primary education in England: a survey by HM Inspectors of Schools*, HMSO, 1978.

DES *Education 5 to 9: an illustrative survey of 80 first schools in England*, HMSO, 1982.

Dean, Joan, 'Study Skills: learning how to learn' in *Education 3—13*, 5, 2, pp. 9—11, 1977.

Friend, Peter and Benjamin, Mary. 'Taking notes' in *Times Educational Supplement*, p. 22, 18.9.81.

Galton, Maurice, *Inside the Primary Classroom*, RKP, 1980.

Galton, Maurice, Progress and Performance in the Primary Classroom, RKP, 1980.

Garland, Roy, *Microcomputers in the Primary School* ed. Roy Garland, Falmer Press, 1982.

Gordon, Cecilia, *Resource organisation in primary schools*, Council for Educational Technology, 1978.

Heather, Pauline, *A study of the use of books and libraries by children in primary schools* (CRUS occasional paper, 11), Sheffield Centre for Research on User Studies, 1984.

Heather, Pauline, *Teaching methods and the use of books and libraries in primary schools: a review*, (CRUS occasional paper, 10). Sheffield Centre for Research on User Studies, 1984.

Irving, Ann, (ed.), *Starting to Teach Study Skills*, (Teaching Matters), Edward Arnold, 1982.

Marland, Michael (ed.), *Information skills in the secondary curriculum: the recommendations of a working group sponsored by the British Library and the Schools Council*, (Schools Council Curriculum Bulletin 9, Methuen Educ.)

Open University Course PME 233., *Mathematics across the curriculum*, O.U. 1979.

Rudduck, Jean, *The sixth form and libraries: problems of access to knowledge* (Library and Information Research Report, 24) British Library Board, 1984.

Schools Council Project, *Developing Children's thinking through Topic Work*, Nottingham. School of Education, University of Nottingham. Project Co-ordinator Trevor Kerry. (In progress).

Somerfield, Muriel, *A framework for reading: creating a policy in the primary school*, for the City of Coventry LEA, Heinemann Educational, 1983.

Southgate, Vera; Arnold, Helen and Johnson, Sandra, *Extending Beginning Reading* (Schools Council Project), Heinemann Educational, 1981.

Webb, Rosemary, *Schools knowledge, pedagogy and development*, (An investigation into information skills in topic work centred on the primary and middle years), Norwich, University of East Anglia. Research in progress for a Ph.D thesis. Projected publication winter 1985.

Teaching Matters

Starting Primary Science

Edited by Megan Hayes

In *Starting Primary Science*, Megan Hayes has assembled a team of contributors who have successfully integrated science into their infant and junior school teaching. We are given vivid examples of how a teacher who has not trained in science can, with a little care and preparation, introduce the subject to children in a thoroughly absorbing way. Exploring the environment, electricity, animals and even household junk can enrich the normal primary diet from a very early age. This book will interest those who already teach science in their primary schools but will be particularly helpful to teachers who have not yet incorporated science into the primary curriculum.

Edward Arnold

Teaching Matters

Micros in the Primary Classroom

Edited by Ron Jones

In *Micros in the Primary Classroom*, Ron Jones and his
contributors offer guidance and practical ideas on how teachers
who are not yet expert in new technology can use the microcomputer as a valuable resource. The authors look particularly
at the ways teachers can use the computer to help their children
develop a skills foundation which will extend well beyond the
primary years. They discuss how the micro can help to exercise
and test skills that are initially taught in a more traditional
way, and describe suitable programs for this, explaining how
they were developed in the first place. They go on to look at
information handling skills, using, among other things,
Victorian census data; problem solving skills in maths using
Logo and the Turtle; problem solving skills using simulations
such as the Mary Rose and Saqarra; and the use of devices
like the BBC Buggy and Bigtrak. Finally, they look at the
opportunities the micro provides for home/school liaison and
consider likely developments for the future. This clear,
accessible and enthusiastic guide will help all primary teachers
approach the micros in their classroom in an informed and
positive way.

Edward Arnold